Martin, Ann, Luke
Jane & Kev

PAPER AMBASSADORS

THE POLITICS OF STAMPS

PAPER AMBASSADORS

THE POLITICS OF STAMPS

DENNIS ALTMAN

ANGUS
& ROBERTSON

A division of HarperCollins*Publishers*

*The publishers acknowledge the assistance of the
following postal agencies: Australia Post, Royal Mail
Stamps and Philately, Canada Post Corporation and the
New Zealand Postal Corporation.*

*Every effort has been made to contact the copyright owners of the
stamps reproduced in this book. Where this has not been possible
the publishers invite them to notify Collins/Angus & Robertson
Publishers Australia.*

AN ANGUS & ROBERTSON BOOK

*First published in Australia in 1991 by
Collins/Angus & Robertson Publishers Australia*

*Collins/Angus & Robertson Publishers Australia
A division of HarperCollins Publishers (Australia) Pty Limited
Unit 4, Eden Park, 31 Waterloo Road, North Ryde
NSW 2113, Australia*

*William Collins Publishers Ltd
31 View Road, Glenfield, Auckland 10, New Zealand*

*Angus & Robertson (UK)
16 Golden Square, London W1R 4BN, United Kingdom*

*National Library of Australia
Cataloguing-in-Publication data:*

*Altman, Dennis.
    Paper Ambassadors
    Includes index.
    ISBN 0 207 16217 4
    1. Postage–stamps. I. Title
769.56*

*Cover and internal illustrations reproduced
with the assistance of La Trobe University.
Typeset in 10pt Baskerville
Printed in Singapore*

* 5   4   3   2   1
95 94 93 92 91*

DEDICATION

In memory of my father, Andrew Altman, without whom I might never have become a stamp collector.

ACKNOWLEDGMENTS

Over the years so many people have contributed to my stamp collection, and hence to this book, that any list would be inadequate. I should single out, above all, my parents; Penny Andrews; Jill Blewett; Andrew Brophy; Margaret Connolly; Susi Loebel; Dan Morgan; Robin Jeffrey; Steven Lawsen; Sonia Neering; Warren Osmond; Phil Parkinson; Nehama Patkin; Barry Prothero; Don Shewey; Garry Wotherspoon and Clive Faro; and the various office people at *Outrage*.

This book began as an idea of then *Pluto* editor Mike Kidron, with whom I had a number of stimulating conversations in London back in 1984/5. Since then my agent, Tim Curnow, was very helpful in placing the book and Norm Rowe encouraged me to proceed. Mary Rennie, Belinda Johnson Lee and Linda Maxwell all played important roles in the production of the book. I am particularly grateful for the support and material provided by Richard Peck, Philatelic Curator at Sydney's Powerhouse Museum. Some people have given me specific help for the book, especially David Boucher, Andrew Foster, Chris Healy, Hector Kinloch, Chris McAuliffe, Martha Macintyre, Senator Chris Puplick, Max Stern, Simon Watney, Paul Watson and — especially — the Reprography Section at La Trobe University.

CONTENTS

INTRODUCTION

WHY LOOK AT STAMPS?

For most people, stamps are objects that are bought after queuing at the post office, used, and discarded. Apart from stamp collectors few people really look at stamps, although almost everyone who is literate will make frequent use of them. Every recognised state — and quite a few unrecognised ones — produces stamps, increasingly far more than are necessary for purely postal purposes. In 1890, a few hundred stamps were issued worldwide; these were small, dignified and sombre in appearance. In 1990 almost 10,000 stamps will be issued, many of them large, garish and multicoloured.

Stamps have rarely been analysed, despite contemporary interest in popular culture as reflected in the growth of semiotics. Perhaps because we all possess, use and receive stamps they are so common they are hardly noticed. This was brought home to me when the great majority of people I asked had no idea that John Lennon had appeared on an Australian stamp in 1988, even though they would almost certainly have

AUSTRALIA 1988

FIJI 1985

come across it as part of a joint Bicentennial issue of four stamps with Great Britain showing the contributions of the two countries to each other. (Shakespeare and the Sydney Opera House appeared on the same stamp.) Almost identical versions of the stamps were issued simultaneously in Britain.

"There is nothing in the world as invisible as monuments" wrote the German author Robert Musil,[1] and in a sense stamps are monuments writ small. Almost no subject is too obscure to appear on stamps. Yet they are both miniature art works and pieces of government propaganda: they can be used to promote sovereignty, celebrate achievement, define national, racial, religious or linguistic identity, portray messages or exhort certain behaviour. Even the most seemingly bland design — one depicting roses, say, or domestic animals — has been deliberately issued by a particular government for a particular purpose.

It is true that it is difficult to read messages into certain designs, those just displaying a numerical value, for example, or those produced by a number of countries using astrological symbols. (Even though the latter would hardly be acceptable to certain orthodoxies, either Christian or Marxist.) But often what appears to be just a pretty picture has a deep significance in the local culture. Stamps of shells — very common from Pacific Island countries — draw on traditional associations; this design from Fiji, for example, shows shells widely used for currency.

In his novel *A Bend in the River*, V.S Naipaul wrote: "Small things can start us off in new ways of thinking, and I was started off by the postage stamps of our area. The British administration gave us beautiful stamps. These stamps depicted local scenes and local things; there was one called 'Arab Dhow'. It was though, in these stamps, a foreigner had said, 'This is what is most striking about this place.' Without that stamp of the dhow I might have taken the dhows for granted. As it was, I learned to look at them. Whenever I saw them tied up at the waterfront I thought of them as something peculiar to our region, quaint, something the foreigner would remark on, something not quite modern and certainly nothing like the liners and cargo ships that berthed in our own modern docks.''[2]

It is the assertion of this book that even if you have never collected stamps in your life, to start really looking at them is, like for Naipaul, to start seeing things anew. What appears on stamps is a message. It is the purpose of this book to decode these messages, and to show how that often ignored piece of coloured paper on the edge of an envelope is part of a picture of the world that governments seek quite consciously to create. In this sense, stamps make up part of what the Australian political scientist Donald Horne has termed "the public culture", namely that set of images and values which are propagated as the taken-for-granted picture of the world.[3]

Unlike postcards, posters or match-books (all of which have their collectors and their documentors) stamps are issued exclusively by governments, or at least entities claiming government status. Hence, it is possible to list all stamps ever issued (the major catalogues — Gibbons in Britain, Scott in the US, Yvert in France — define what is acceptable to stamp collectors, although occasionally one lists issues the others do not consider legitimate). The total to date comes to about a quarter of a million stamps, produced by up to 600 authorities, of which the Soviet Union has produced the largest single number.

Increasingly ordinary mail sees stamps replaced by franking machines, particularly common in the United States

KENYA, UGANDA
AND TANGANYIKA 1935

and France, and letters themselves are being displaced by electronic means of communication. Nonetheless, the number of stamps issued each year continues to increase, with countries most active in developing other forms of communication, such as the United States and Japan, as profligate in their stamp-issuing policies as anyone else. Clearly stamps have become useful ideological and cultural artifacts and a means for governments to both promote certain images at home and abroad and increase revenue. It is the latter motivation that is increasingly dominant and explains the vast number of stamps currently issued. Many small countries rely heavily on stamps to earn hard currency and their designs reflect this, but even large countries are concerned with the image their stamps present to their citizens and the outside world, and with the sales revenue from collectors who, after all, buy stamps without expecting any postal service in return.

1. Quoted by Marina Warner, *Monuments and Maidens*, Wiedenfeld and Nicholson, London, 1985, p. 21.
2. V.S. Naipaul, *A Bend in the River*, Deutsch, London, 1979, p. 22.
3. D. Horne, *The Public Culture*, Pluto, London, 1986.

C H A P T E R   O N E

WHO ISSUED WHAT AND WHEN?

The First Stamp

Before the invention of the postage stamp, mail was paid for on delivery. This required complicated bookkeeping and allowed large numbers of addressees to refuse to accept delivery of letters. Stamps were a simple way of ensuring that all postage was prepaid, thus paving the way for cheap and universal postage charges. The real significance of the postage stamp was that it revolutionised the means of paying for postage.

Stamps first came into being in 1840 when the Industrial Revolution was already well underway in Great Britain, and the volume of mail was increasing correspondingly. Like the telegraph, postage stamps were part of the enormous growth of communications and transport during the 19th century. At least one author claims that 1840, the year of the first stamp, was also the beginning of a forty-year era of "the triumph of progress". [1]

The first adhesive stamp to be used for postal purposes appeared in Great Britain, following a suggestion of Sir Rowland Hill. Since the establishment of a national postal service in 1660, there had existed a range of tariffs, depending on distance and the number of pages in a letter, paid for by the receiver. Hill proposed a low, standard rate of postage and payment in advance. He was able to show that the real cost to the postal service was in handling, not in distance carried. The invention of the adhesive stamp, which could be postmarked to show use, made possible a system of a uniform rate for mail delivery paid for by the sender. [2]

The "Penny Black", the first stamp issued, bore a stylised portrait of Queen Victoria, staring regally to the left, as does Queen Elizabeth on current British issues, and was valid for all letters of half an ounce carried in Britain. A second stamp of twopence was also issued for other rates. There was some feeling at the time that licking the back of the Queen's head was undignified, if not potentially treasonous. A similar attitude still remains in Japan, which does not portray royalty on its stamps (until 1947 all Japanese stamps bore the stylised chrysanthemum which is the symbol of the Emperor). Spain and Sicily sought a different solution to royal sensitivities by using a postmark that would frame, rather than obliterate, the portrait of the monarch on their early issues. Black was an unfortunate colour, as it was difficult to see postmarks, and the following year it was replaced by a brown stamp.

By 1898 the penny rate had become Empire wide. This was commemorated by Canada with a stamp showing a map of the world, with the Empire in red, bearing the inscription, "We hold a vaster Empire than has been." (As the stamp also carried the inscription "Xmas 1898", it has the distinction of being the first ever Christmas stamp.)

Having initiated the whole idea, Britain has never identified its stamps with the country's name (true of a

CANADA 1898

number of other states in the 19th century) but has instead used the sovereign's head. This was stylised and reduced in size on commemorative stamps in 1966 under the direction of the then Postmaster General Tony Benn. Benn, a leading figure on the left of the British Labour Party for 30 years, was a major influence on the growth and scope of British issues, although he failed in his attempt to remove the Queen's head altogether from stamps. His diaries contain a large number of references to the battle he waged against Buckingham Palace to change the design of British stamps, and as some insight into the Palace's interest in stamps he quotes Harold Wilson as telling him of an audience with the Queen, "We spent ten minutes on Rhodesia and an hour and five minutes on stamps."[3] Despite some indignation from traditionalists, who might have remembered George VI's warning to Kenneth Clark that, "One day they'll take my head off", Benn's changes have remained, and a diminutive profile of the monarch still identifies stamps as British. With the proliferation of royal stamps (to be discussed later) Queen Elizabeth II has undoubtedly appeared on many more stamps than any other person.

GREAT BRITAIN 1966

The Expansion of Stamps

The expansion of stamps reflected the growing needs of commerce and the spread of new forms of transportation during the nineteenth century. The 1820s and 1830s had seen the introduction of railways and steamships, and with them the possibility of carrying mail over long distances and with greater reliability than ever before. All of this increased the advantages of a system of prepaid postage. The British innovation was to become virtually universal very quickly.

Urged on by an astute consul in London, Brazil was the first country to follow the British lead and in 1843 issued its own official postage stamp of an oval design which became known as the "Bull's Eye".

The United States legislated for standard postage in 1845, but failed to issue stamps for two years; in the interim a number of local postmasters issued their own, now much sought after by collectors. Other early issues came from the Swiss cantons of Zurich and Geneva, soon followed by some of the British colonies. Early issues from Mauritius (1847) and Bermuda (1848) show the way in which the diffusion of stamps tended to follow the Imperial steamship routes, which were constantly expanded and improved throughout the century.

Not surprisingly, stamps were first adopted in Europe by the more industrialised countries (France, Belgium and Bavaria all produced them in 1849). By 1860, stamps had appeared in most parts of the British Empire and Europe, in Liberia, and in a number of countries in the Americas. Some of Germany's first stamps came from the princely house of Thurn and Taxis, whose carriers (20,000 of them in the 17th century) and ensignia of yellow trumpets were known throughout Europe. In 1867 Prussia took over their remaining services , and a few years later integrated them into those of the new Imperial Germany.

In 1863, prompted by the US Postmaster General, Montgomery Blair, the first international postal conference was held in Paris to discuss ways of improving and simplifying international postal deliveries. It was Germany's first postmaster, Dr Heinrich von Stephan, who was largely responsible for the foundation of the Universal Postal Union (UPU) in 1875, the oldest extant international government organisation, which ensures international postal deliveries.

The Congress of Berne, which established the UPU, laid down one of the most striking examples to date of international co-operation, namely that for the purposes of postal communication all member countries form, in effect, a single territory. Thus each member is bound to carry the mail of all other member states with the same speed and efficiency it provides for its own and to deliver mail without cost. This is on the assumption that letters generally lead to responses and hence there would be a balancing out of costs. (This has not proven to be the case, however, and there are now provisions for some payment where one country delivers many more letters than it generates.)

To make this workable the convention also set certain basic postal rates for international mail and laid down certain conditions of size and weight. There were also agreements covering money orders, parcels and registered letters. Membership of the UPU was originally largely European (with colonies being covered via the membership of the colonial power). Before their government joined the UPU in 1928, Afghanis sending letters out of the country had to use Indian stamps in addition to their own. Today however the UPU, which is now an agency of the United Nations, is the most universal of all international agencies, and has considerable expertise in assisting poorer countries to develop their postal systems. Meetings of the UPU Congress, every five years, are almost always an occasion for special stamp issues by the host country. The UPU office in Berne issues its own stamps for official use.

FIJI 1949

COLOMBIA 1974

By the time of the establishment of the UPU steamship and railroads meant that letters were travelling around

GERMANY 1899

FINLAND 1930

the world on modern forms of transport, and by the end of the century even such isolated states as Nepal and Ethiopia were producing stamps. The 20th-century expectation that for a small sum of money a letter could be sent from virtually anywhere in the world and be guaranteed delivery almost anywhere else had been established.

Early stamp issues tended to bear either the sovereign's head, as used by Belgium, Portugal and Thailand; a numerical design, as with Brazil and Japan; or a national symbol, either a coat of arms, as in Germany and Austria, or allegorical figures such as a dragon for China and Ceres for France. (Ceres, the goddess of grain, was displaced within several years by the image of the Emperor Napoleon III but brought back after the fall of the Third Empire in 1870. She was the first in a line of allegorical women such as ''Marianne'' and, currently, ''Liberty'' who have been used on French definitives.) In 1899 Germany used the image of a woman entitled ''Germania'', allegedly modelled on the Kaiser's mistress.

Symbols used by countries on their first stamps included the sun from Uruguay (1856), a bull's head from Moldavia (1858) and a mermaid-like figure from Liberia (1860). Finland, which although part of Imperial Russia issued its own stamps after 1856, showed a heraldic lion on its first stamps. As Russian control was tightened at the end of the 19th century, these were replaced with stamps very similar to those of Russia, but after independence in 1917 the lion motif returned. Several countries showed national heroes, such as George Washington and Benjamin Franklin in the United States. Chile showed Christopher Columbus and Mexico showed the nationalist leader, Miguel Hidalgo. Canada, with a beaver, and Western Australia, with a swan, inaugurated the ever-popular animal motif, while El Salvador's first stamp (1867) showed a volcano.

Stamps for Empires

Given the British origin of postage stamps, it is not surprising that British colonies were among the earliest to make use of the new device. These stamps were sometimes designed and produced in the colonies themselves, leading to such curiosities as the typewritten stamps produced on sermon paper by a missionary in Uganda (and now worth hundreds of pounds, if available), the typeset stamps printed locally by *The Fiji Times,* and the very rare, locally produced early stamps from British Guiana. Although portraits of Queen Victoria were the most common design, there is a surprising variety in these early Imperial stamps. The 1860 issue for New Brunswick included a locomotive, a steamship and a portrait of the then Postmaster General, Charles Connell, who was forced to withdraw the stamps and resign after a public outcry at his egotism.[4] It is now a generally accepted policy in Britain that stamps not show living persons other than members of the Royal family, a restraint not adhered to by most other countries. There were however, several famous British exceptions in the 19th century when stamps were issued for use in the besieged town of Mafeking during the Boer War and portraits of both Cadet Sergeant-Major Warner Goodyear and General Baden Powell (later to be commemorated on large numbers of stamps as the founder of the Boy Scouts) were used.

Other empires used a common design for all their colonies. The first issue of French stamps, in 1849, included stamps intended for use throughout the French Empire, and Germany, Spain and Portugal all produced stamps with common designs for use in all their colonies. (Shown here are the German "yacht" and the Portuguese "Ceres".) Even after France began issuing separate stamps for various colonies, common designs were often used. At various stages stamps were issued for use in all parts of the French Empire, ranging

CAMEROUN 1900

ANGOLA 1914

CAMEROUN 1942

GAMBIA 1946

BELGIAN CONGO 1931

from those of Napoleon III to the Free French issues during World War II, but more common were designs with only the name of the colony changed, as for the 1931 International Colonial Exhibition. Britain adopted a similar policy to commemorate certain Imperial events, such as the Silver Jubilee of George V or Victory in World War II. More recently, as we shall see, Royal events have been commemorated with common issues by a large number of British dependencies and dominions.

The advantages of separate stamps, both as ways of satisfying local sentiment and as convenient sources of revenue, meant that each colony, even where there was almost total control from the metropolis, eventually came to issue its own stamps. Some British possessions have come relatively late into the stamp-issuing world. The southern Atlantic Ocean island of Tristan da Cunha (population under 500) has issued stamps regularly only since 1952. Until then it apparently managed quite well without its own stamps, although some missionary-produced labels existed.

The stamps of the various European empires have a strange mix of imperial and local themes. British stamp designs for her largest colony, India, were in marked contrast

ERITREA 1930

PAPUA 1932

The first stamps of the so-called "Independent State of the Congo" (now Zaire) bore the portrait of King Leopold II of Belgium — not surprisingly as the colony was virtually his private domain. After the government of Belgium took direct control in 1908, the authorities adopted the practice of showing scenic views and scenes of native life, including some quite striking portraits of "native women". However they also managed to include numerous issues highlighting the benefits of Belgian rule, including one issue showing Queen Astrid with local children.

Similarly, themes of "native life" were common on other colonial issues, especially African, in the period between the two World Wars. It is not accidental that this period saw the flourishing of anthropology and a European fascination with "the savage races" whom their colonial empires had "tamed". European imperialism was on the defensive in the years after World War II with the growth of independence movements in Asia and Africa, so colonial authorities tended to look to safer subjects for exotica, such as flora and fauna. Today, of course, one sees a reappearance of some of the old "native" themes in stamps from independent African and Pacific countries, keen to reclaim indigenous culture from the voyeurism of colonial rulers.

TOGO 1970

to the pictorial issues of the French colonies, or even the stamps in some of the West Indian and African colonies of the British Empire. The themes of the stamps were overwhelmingly imperial and even those few issues that were pictorial included symbols of British rule, such as the Viceroy's House and the Victoria Memorial, Calcutta, alongside traditional

INDIA 1936

Indian buildings such as the Taj Mahal and the Golden Temple, Amritsar. Clearly the authorities felt that stamps that in any way encouraged the already powerful forces of Indian nationalism should be avoided. At the same time, they also wished to avoid too much offence to this growing nationalism, and India did not take part in Empire issues for the 1937 Coronation of George VI (although a portrait of the King dominated all Indian stamps until Independence in 1947). Local rulers did, of course, appear on the issues of the various feudatory states, where, as in French Indo-China the colonial rulers sought to cement their rule through local dynasties. Stamps were issued showing the hereditary rulers of Cambodia, Annam and Laos.

Imperialism produced exotic political entities, each with its own stamps. As Stephen Leacock wrote in a piece subtitled *The Habitable Globe as Seen through the Eyes of the Juvenile Collector*, "The principal countries of the world are Cochin-China, the Gilbert Islands, Somali Land, the Gaboon, the Cameroons, Nankipu, Johore, and Whango-Whango. Alongside of these great stamp areas are others of less importance, whose stamps are seldom if ever worth more than four cents, such as the United States, Great Britain, Canada, France etc."[5]

The expansion of Europe into the rest of the world reached its peak in the second half of the 19th century and produced an extraordinary range of stamps. Often a postal administration was one of the ways in which colonial control was exercised, so that, for example, some of the first stamps issued in China were for use by the separate postal administrations of Russia, Britain, Germany, the United States, France and Italy. Equally, Italy established the right to operate its own post offices throughout the Ottoman Empire in the early years of this century, overprinting its stamps for use in such places as Jerusalem, Smyrna and Constantinople. By the time the Treaty of Lausanne recognised Turkey's independence in 1923, ten powers had post offices in the country, including, if only briefly, Egypt, Romania and Poland.[6]

The Rise of New States

The consolidation of nation-states out of former small countries and colonies was a feature of the 19th century and was reflected in the disappearance of a number of stamp producing places as with the unification of Italy and Germany. The British success in the Boer War, which forced the establishment of the Union of South Africa in 1910, meant the loss of separate stamps for each of the colonies, including rarities such as primitive hand-stamped issues for the short-lived Vrijheid (New Republic) which became part of Natal. This disappearance was not always the rule, however. Bavaria continued to issue its own stamps until 1920, 50 years after it joined the German Empire, and Bosnia-Herzegovina, now part of Yugoslavia, issued its own distinctive stamps even

BOSNIA AND HERZEGOVINA 1906

while it was part of the Austro-Hungarian Empire. One can also find stamps from British Colombia and Prince Edward Island, which did not join the Dominion of Canada until the 1870s and, in theory, the stamps of Newfoundland, which remained a separate dominion until 1949, remain valid for postal use in Canada.

It would be possible to assemble a collection of stamps designed to illustrate all the shifts in sovereignty of the 20th century, as one of the first acts of almost every new state is to issue its own stamps. Such a collection would illustrate the confusion that often attended periods such as the break-up of the Austro-Hungarian, Russian and Turkish Empires at the end of World War I. The use of plebiscites to resolve the nationality of certain disputed territories meant the issue of a number of temporary stamps (often by overprinting existing stamps) for use in places such as Carinthia (which became part of Austria), Marienwerder (incorporated into Germany) and the Saar, which was administered for 15 years by France under control of the League of Nations and returned to Germany in 1935. (There was a similar French occupation after World War II, and a further plebescite returned it to West Germany in 1957.) Stamps from both periods have a considerable philatelic appeal.

One can see the complex history of Yugoslavia reflected in numerous stamp issues. Immediately after World War I and the dissolution of the Austro-Hungarian Empire, there were separate stamps for Croatia, Slovenia and Bosnia-Herzegovina for several years before they united with Serbia (which had issued its own stamps since 1866) to form the Kingdom of the Serbs, Croats and Slovenes (1921). In 1929 this became in turn the Kingdom of Yugoslavia.

In similar ways the break-up of the colonial empires in Asia, Africa, the Caribbean and the Pacific after

Further complications arose on the Yugoslav border with Italy, where the town of Fiume was disputed between the two states. An Italian invasion in 1919 was led by the Italian poet Gabriele d'Annunzio, and a free state was proclaimed which was incorporated into Italy in 1924. It was renamed Rijeka and became part of Yugoslavia after World War II. Similar disputes over control of the Adriatic port of Trieste and the surrounding territory of Venezia Giulia followed World War II: the territory was divided into two zones, both issuing their own stamps until they were incorporated into Italy and Yugoslavia respectively in 1954. The illustrations show a 1923 stamp of Fiume overprinted to mark its incorporation into Italy; an Italian stamp overprinted with the symbol of the Allied Military Government which occupied Zone A of Trieste after World War II; and a stamp of the Yugoslav military government of Zone B.

TRIESTE (Italian) 1947;
TRIESTE (Yugoslav) 1952;
FIUME 1923

World War II have produced new stamp-issuing states and frequent changes in stamp issues. The British withdrawal from its Indian Empire saw the emergence of modern India, Pakistan, Burma (Myanmar) and Ceylon (renamed Sri Lanka in 1972), and paved the way for the end of European empires in Asia; today only Hong Kong remains, and it will revert to China before the end of the century. The 1950s saw major colonial wars against the French in Algeria and Indo-China, and independence for Malaysia and Ghana (formerly the Gold Coast). In 1960, 17 African countries were granted independence, which meant the end of most direct French rule and in the following few years the British withdrew from their remaining African colonies (with some difficulty in Rhodesia after a revolt by white settlers). The Portuguese Empire ended with the independence of its African colonies in 1975, and Britain withdrew from most of its remaining Pacific and Caribbean island colonies.

All these shifts are reflected in a proliferation of new stamp issues. New names appear, and various attempts at joint issues come and go. The turbulent politics of East Africa can be seen reflected in the union of Tanganyika and Zanzibar to form Tanzania; in joint issues of the former British East African states, since abandoned in favour of separate stamps; in the invasion of Uganda by Kenya — which saw all current Ugandan stamps overprinted with the words: "Uganda Liberated 1979" — as well as in the various stamp issues surrounding the creation of Zimbabwe out of the former British colony of Southern Rhodesia and separatist revolts in Zaire (the former Belgian Congo).

While many of the states that issued stamps in the 19th century have since been amalgamated and enlarged, new small states have arisen since World War II. San Marino and Monaco are the oldest of these countries that proclaim their Ruritanian sovereignty through separate stamps, increasingly geared to collectors. There is a precedent for some of the tiny

KENYA, UGANDA AND TANZANIA 1971

states, whose garish stamps now dominate stamp shop windows, in the Indian feudatory states or the Greek Islands which issued stamps in earlier times. Particularly notorious for the number of stamps they issued, were the various sheikdoms that formed the United Arab Emirates in 1971, and some of the island states of the South Pacific and the Caribbean. The number of stamp-producing states in the 1980s was around 260, and more appear each year. As we shall see, the right to issue separate stamps raises complex questions of sovereignty, in which a mixture of commercial and political expediency is often involved.

Regional Issues

Governments have often allowed the issue of stamps for regions or states with only limited autonomy. While this is usually either to placate nationalist sentiments or as an extra source of revenue, some local stamps result from genuine postal needs. Perhaps the best example of such regional stamps are the "Zemstvos" from 19th-century Russia. These stamps were produced by rural district governments for use within their own territories, or in conjunction with Imperial Russian stamps for wider delivery. Under British rule many of the various princely states of India issued their own stamps, usually limited to use within their own boundaries. Most were restricted to one or two issues, and there are a few, for example those from Hyderabad or Travancore, with quite striking designs. Some states, such as Gwalior and Jind, used overprints of Indian stamps.

Today a fair number of regional stamp issues exist. Although the regions of Britain have far less autonomy than Canadian provinces or Australian states — which do not issue separate stamps — there are separate definitive issues for Scotland, Wales and Northern Ireland, while Guernsey, Jersey and the Isle of Man issue a constant stream of stamps aimed at tourists and collectors. Similarly, the Danish-ruled Faroe Islands and the Finnish province of the Aland Islands produce their own stamps, and each state of Malaysia produces its own stamps, in addition to the common national issues. The special status of West Berlin has been recognised by its own stamp issues, sometimes using the same design as those of West Germany.

On the other hand, areas that one might expect to issue their own stamps are sometimes denied them. In general those parts of the remaining French Empire classified as departments (French Guiana, Guadeloupe and Reunion) do not issue their own stamps. The United States does not issue separate stamps for Puerto Rico, Guam or the Virgin Islands. Nevertheless, changes in the status of the United States' Pacific Ocean Trust Territories of Palau and the Marshall Islands have been reflected in separate stamps since 1983 and, until it was handed back to Panama, there were separate stamps for the US-governed Panama Canal Zone. In the same way Niue, a Pacific island dependent on New Zealand, Norfolk Island and the Cocos and Christmas Islands, administered by Australia, have long had their own stamps. As demands for autonomy escalate within the various republics of the Soviet Union, it may not be long before we see separate stamp issues for Estonia and Armenia.

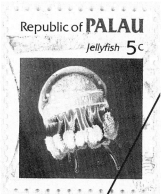

FEDERATED STATES OF MICRONESIA 1988; PALAU 1988

Conflicts over Sovereignty

In the above cases the central government itself issues the regional stamps; in other cases stamps are produced by regions as a declaration of independence. Sometimes it seems as if every conflict produces its own postal administrations, from the American Civil War (when the Confederacy issued stamps, in addition to large numbers of provisional issues by local Southern postmasters, who loyally refused to use stamps produced in Washington once the War had begun) to the stamps of Biafra and Katanga in this century. Just before Biafran separatists were crushed by Nigerian troops in 1970, a stamp, showing an African child in chains, was released overprinted with the words: "SAVE BIAFRA 9th JAN 1970". It was not, however, put on sale in Biafra. In the Turkish areas of Cyprus a separate postal system, with local labels, preceded the Turkish military intervention in 1974. Since then, the enmity between Greek and Turkish Cypriots has been fought out on stamps — the Turks portraying their "liberation fighters" and the Greeks invoking the support of the United Nations (see page 22).

KATANGA 1961

    At times there is such a total breakdown of government control that there is apparently no longer a recognised postal administration in a position to issue stamps. This frequently seems to have been the situation over the past decade in Cambodia and Lebanon. One report in 1986 spoke of stamps bearing the inscription "Islamic republic of Lebanon" which were being used in the south of the country, though were not recognised internationally.

    The Bolshevik Revolution in Russia not only produced its reflection in stamp design, but also led to a number of opposition groups producing their own regional issues in

BIAFRA 1968

CYPRUS (Greek) 1974; (Turkish) 1983

GEORGIA 1919; BRITISH OCCUPIED BATUM 1920

Siberia, Georgia, Armenia, Azerbaijan and the Ukraine before they were incorporated into the Soviet Union. Allied intervention on the side of the White Russians is shown in stamps issued during the British occupation of Batum, once known as Petra, on the Black Sea. The Ukraine and the Transcaucasian Federation issued stamps as late as 1923, and the last area in the Soviet Union to issue separate stamps was the North Mongolian province of Tuva, nominally independent until 1944, whose brightly coloured and oddly shaped stamps were staples of many pre-war collections.

All these stamps were presumably useable for at least some postal purposes and accepted as valid even in the absence of international recognition of their source. Good examples are the stamps of the various South African "homelands". When the Transkei began producing stamps in 1977, the Stanley Gibbons catalogue claimed they were recognised *de facto* for carriage of mail, even in the absence of international recognition of the Transkei. Similar issues by Bophuthatswana, Ciskei and Venda have been used to proclaim the independence of the homelands and their attractiveness to tourists (see stamp at right). These stamps cannot be imported unused into some countries as part of their economic sanctions against South Africa, just as earlier stamps proclaiming the unilateral independence of Rhodesia were banned in Britain (although they were apparently accepted by postal authorities for the delivery of mail.

Occasionally, rebel governments or governments in exile will issue stamps, sometimes for use in areas under their control, as in the case of the National Front for the Liberation of South Vietnam, or to win overseas support and funding. Stamps were produced for the breakaway Indonesian province of the South Moluccas in the 1950s and the International Stamp Exchange Corporation of Miami Beach claims to have raised $2.5 million for Afghan rebels by issuing "stamps", presumably with no expectation that they would be used for postal purposes. In 1986 the company announced it would do the same for the Angolan Unita rebels of Jonas Savimbi. Similar propaganda "stamps" were produced in the 1980s by the Solidarity movement in Poland and they received considerable publicity. In the west collectors were attracted by designs showing Solidarity protests and honouring Pope John Paul II, George Orwell (author of the antitotalitarian classics *Animal Farm* and *1984*), Ronald Reagan and Soviet dissident physicist Andrei Sakharov. Presumably no one in Angola or Poland seriously sought to post letters using these "stamps".

VENDA 1986

A peaceful example of the issue of stamps as part of disputes over sovereignty is from the Antarctic, where there is no full international recognition of the claims of various countries to parts of the continent. The first Antarctic stamp was issued in 1911 by New Zealand which overprinted two of its then current stamps "VICTORIA LAND" for use by the Scott Expedition. Since the 1950s Britain, France, Australia and New Zealand have all issued stamps for the

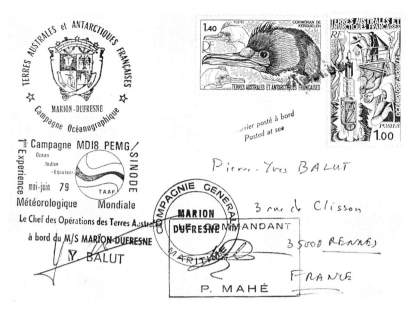

FRENCH SOUTHERN AND ANTARCTIC TERRITORIES 1979

areas they claim, even though their immediate postal use is limited to the couple of scientific stations the various countries maintain in the Antarctic. (However, the French stamps are also valid for certain islands in the South Indian Ocean, while the Australian Antarctic issues are valid for ordinary postage within Australia.) In the absence of international recognition, the creation of special stamp-issuing authorities represents one of the ways in which the various contending powers seek to assert their claims to sovereignty. Argentina and Chile have both issued stamps depicting their claims to portions of the continent.

1. B. Youngerman, "World History", *The World Almanach & Book of Facts*, Newspaper Enterprise Association, New York, 1985, p. 503.
2. For more detail see Neil Grant and Peter Womersley, *Collecting Stamps*, Granada, London, 1980.
3. T. Benn, *Out of the Wilderness*, Hutchinson, London, 1987 p. 344.
4. See J. Mackay, *Commonwealth Stamp Design 1840–1965*, British Museum, London, 1965.
5. S. Leacock, "The Stamp-Album World", *Short Circuits*, Dodd, Mead, New York, 1928, p. 90.
6. D. Reid, "The Symbolism of Postage Stamps", *Journal of Contemporary History*, vol. 19, no.2, 1984, p. 233.

VARIETIES OF STAMPS

The First Commemoratives

Collectors usually distinguish between "definitives" — stamps that are issued for normal postal purposes and may remain on sale for some time (Norway used the same numerical and posthorn designs for almost a century) — and "commemoratives". In 1871 Peru issued a stamp to mark the 20th anniversary of the first railway in the country, from Lima to Callao, generally regarded as the first commemorative stamp. In 1876 the United States produced a special stamped envelope to mark the Centennial Exhibition, and the first commemorative series came from New South Wales (Australia), which celebrated the centenary of British settlement in 1888 with an issue of ten stamps showing animals, views of Sydney and both Captains Cook and Phillip. By the end of the century, special stamps had appeared to commemorate the Antwerp Exhibition, Columbus's "discovery" of the Americas, the

NORWAY 1937

Silver Jubilee of King Carol of Romania, the Silver Wedding of the Japanese Emperor and the first modern Olympics in Greece.

The present flood of stamps owes a great deal to the growing number of events that are considered fit and proper subjects for commemoration on stamps. Among the earliest subjects were royal events and international exhibitions, very popular themes in the first several decades of this century. One can see the evolution of what is considered appropriate subject matter very clearly in the case of Great Britain, which for a long time was more restrained than other countries in issuing stamps, including some of its own colonies. Britain did not issue its first commemorative stamps until 1924 — 84 years after its first stamp — a series of four for the Empire Exhibition at Wembley. These stamps bore a large portrait of George V and a lion and were followed, in 1929, by stamps for the ninth UPU meeting in London, showing St George and the dragon alongside the same image of the King. For almost the next 30 years in Britain commemorative stamps were restricted to major events, often royal. The coronations of George VI and Elizabeth II, the Olympic Games of 1948, the Festival of Britain in 1951 and the World Scout Jamboree of 1957 all had their special stamps.

In Britain during the 1950s, a greater number of commemorative issues began to appear — since 1960 at least two issues a year — and their scope widened. In addition to early issues for royal, parliamentary and postal anniversaries, stamps appeared for other international gatherings, and to commemorate a growing range of British "great men", including Shakespeare, Churchill and the pioneer surgeon Joseph Lister. (It took until 1968 for the first "great woman", suffragette Emmeline Pankhurst, to appear on a stamp.) Stamps were issued showing British landscapes and birds (1966), wild flowers and paintings (1967), the first British

Christmas stamp (1966), scenes from childrens' books, movie actors and motor cars — the whole range, in fact, of modern stamp themes. Even today Britain is one of the more restrained countries. It will still not portray any living person on its stamps, other than members of the Royal family, but the rapid growth in subject matter over the past three decades is a sign of how the official understanding of stamps has changed.

One can trace a similar evolution in other stamp-issuing countries. The United States, for example, in addition to large numbers of stamps emphasising the triumphal history and settlement of the country, issued a number of early commemoratives for major exhibitions: the Trans-Mississippi Exposition, Omaha (1898), the Pan American Exposition, Buffalo (1901), the International Exposition, St Louis (1904) and so on. It was not until the 1930s and the Presidency of Franklin Roosevelt, that less grandiose themes began to appear on its stamps, with issues for Mother's Day and national parks.

The inter-war years, in general, saw a large expansion in the subject matter of stamps. Yugoslavia celebrated both the European rowing championship in 1932 and the 11th conference of PEN, an international association of writers, the following year. Ecuador commemorated new railway lines and the centenary of Darwin's visit to the Galapagos Islands, which it owned. Some European countries issued stamps with black borders as mourning stamps, usually for royalty.

Each country has defined what is "fit and proper" for commemorative stamps somewhat differently. In almost all cases, however, commemorative stamps now outnumber definitives, and, as I shall go on to argue, there is a widely agreed perception of what kinds of subjects are appropriate for stamps. Official definitions of culture and the state show uncomfortable similarities between the stamps of, for example, Iran and the United States, Cuba and the Vatican.

GREAT BRITAIN 1985; 1979

NEW SOUTH WALES 1897

Stamps for Charities

New South Wales also led the way with stamps bearing a surcharge to support charity, by issuing two stamps in 1897 to raise money for a home for consumptives. The stamps sold for one shilling and two shillings sixpence each, but with a postal value of only one penny and twopence halfpenny, a considerable donation for the time. The idea of using surcharges to raise money for charity became widespread during World War I, with issues for war orphans, widows and even, from Sweden, clothing for reservists. During the 1930s, a number of countries produced stamps for unemployment relief and Belgium issued a particularly large number of charity stamps, in some years a majority of all issues. During World War II Nazi Germany resorted to increasing numbers of such issues to raise money for causes such as Hitler's "Culture Fund" and the Labour Corps.

There exist a number of long-lived annual charity issues, such as France's for the Red Cross, Switzerland's and the Netherlands' for youth, and New Zealand's for health, used to support children's camps (see right). When Tony Benn introduced Christmas stamps to Britain in 1966, he suggested that they bear a charity surcharge, but this was not acceptable to the Treasury. Britain produced a charity issue for the handicapped in 1975 and several charity Christmas stamps in 1989. Other countries have been less restrained. Turkey has produced stamps to provide money for the Red Crescent, child welfare and the Florence Nightingale Foundation, while France has collected, via stamps, for the Fresh Air Crusade, World Refugee Year and unemployed intellectuals. These last, issued between 1937 and 1939, showed, appropriately, cultural figures such as Anatole France, Balzac and Claude Debussy. Luxembourg also produced a series in 1935

GERMANY 1939

FRANCE 1938

NEW ZEALAND 1942

showing presumably unemployed teachers, surgeons and journalists etc.

Obviously only certain charities will receive the official imprimatur that comes with an official stamp surcharge. In some cases such stamps become disguised forms of taxation. Between 1911 and 1928, Portugal issued a number of charity tax stamps which had to be used on letters posted on special days. The profits were to go to causes such as "the poor" and the building of a memorial to the Marquess of Pombal, a major 18th-century statesman who rebuilt Lisbon after the earthquake of 1755.

Stamps for Special Purposes

Stamps have been issued to provide for a whole range of specialised purposes. There have been stamps produced for use on parcels, for express letters, for "personal delivery", for newspapers, for government departments and so on. Germany had a special series for use by Nazi Party officials. New

SPAIN 1916

Zealand has long issued special stamps for use by the Government Life Insurance Office. Belgium has produced stamps for carrying parcels by the (private) rail system and Italy issued special stamps on several occasions for use in the pneumatic mail system that existed in (literally, beneath) a number of Italian cities. There exist special stamps for Sunday delivery, and, even odder, Belgium for a period before World War I produced stamps with tabs which had to be detached to ensure delivery on Sunday. In 1921 the Netherlands issued special stamps for mail carried in unsinkable safes aboard ships bound for the Indies and, in 1939, Argentina produced stamps for the mailing of recorded messages, intended for use by the illiterate. Special stamps for use by the military have been common. Spain has issued stamps for use by parliamentarians and in the 1930s, the Dominican Republic required a special stamp on mail addressed to the President of the Republic.

"Postage due" stamps — added by the post office for delivery of insufficiently stamped mail — are very common. Over the last few years FRAMA — a Swiss invention of specially printed labels that take the place of stamps and which are available from automatic vending machines — have come into use in a number of countries. So far they strike me as extremely uninteresting objects but there is already a vogue for collecting them. As one dealer put it, in the over-heated prose typical of many stamp advertisements, "...these electronically printed stamps are a sure pointer into the future. You print these stamps for whatever face value you need. There are already Self-Service Postal Stations around where you do your postings without the help of a postal clerk... The THINK-ING PERSON (Let's hope you are one) is already having a collection going... It is not too late to start!" [1]

There are a number of "stamps" that, though issued by, or available at, post offices have no postal purpose at all. The best known examples are the United States "duck stamps" which are, in fact, licences to hunt waterfowl printed to look like stamps.

Airmail Stamps

Most common among specialised stamps are those intended for use on airmail — now so common that they are rarely regarded as special issues. Early airmail stamps are very popular among collectors for they usually bear designs directly related to the history of aviation. (A variant is to collect covers, which may include details of air routes taken. In rare cases, there may be evidence of crashes or other mishaps, where letters were retrieved and delivered complete with explanations of the accident detailed on the envelope.)

The first airmail stamps were issued in 1917, when Italy overprinted "Express" stamps for use on flights between Rome and Turin, and Naples and Palermo, Sicily. Airmail stamps were also particularly popular in the Americas with Colombia and the United States issuing stamps for airmail as far back as 1918, the time of the first airmail flights, and marking various achievements in extending airmail services throughout the 1920s and 1930s. Britain never had separate airmail stamps, but they were issued by all the dominions. Newfoundland, which was geographically crucial in early attempts to cross the Atlantic by plane, commemorated a number of early flights on its stamps, some of which are now extremely sought after. The use of Zeppelins for carrying postage in the 1930s produced a number of special stamps from countries in both Europe and the Americas. Many of these stamps are now rarities because they were only used on Zeppelin flights.

GERMANY 1936

UNITED STATES OF AMERICA 1988

Increasingly, first-class mail is carried automatically by air and many countries do not issue specific airmail stamps. The United States, however, has retained such stamps, most of which bear designs specifically linked to the history of aviation.

WESTERN SAMOA 1942

Overprints and Surcharges

Large numbers of stamps exist that have been overprinted, most often because of a sudden change in postal rates or a change in sovereignty before new stamps can be issued. During the hyper-inflation in Germany in the 1920s, stamps were overprinted to keep pace with changes in the value of money. New values were expressed in thousands, even millions, of marks. In several cases portraits on stamps have been overprinted when political shifts made this expedient. When Reza Pahlavi overthrew the Shah of Persia in 1925, he ordered that all stamps bearing the portrait of his predecessor could be used only if the image was completely obliterated. The most unusual case of an overprint, however, may well be the American stamps from the 1920s overprinted "Kans"(as) and "Nebr"(aska). Hold-ups of post offices in these states had become so frequent that the overprints were designed to prevent stamps being taken out of the state, and thus reduce the chance of the robbers making use of them.

Private and Local Stamps

The regulations of the UPU prevent stamps being produced for postal services by private companies but such stamps do in fact exist, from the Wells Fargo and Suez Canal Companies in the 19th century, to stamps issued by Lansa and Avianca Airlines in the 1950s with the authorisation of the government of Colombia. (Private and semi-private stamps were particularly common in the early days of airmail.) Between 1890 and 1917, the British South Africa Company produced stamps for use in Rhodesia, just as the Mozambique Company produced stamps for parts of Portuguese East Africa until 1940. In general, however, postal services are considered the monopoly of governments, and privately produced stamps usually have no validity for international postal purposes.

This has not prevented various individuals and localities producing "stamps", often for sale to credulous collectors or, at best, used for carriage to the nearest government post office (such as the stamps, denominated in puffins, that come from the privately owned British Isle of Lundy in the Bristol Channel and which can be used for carriage to the nearest mainland post office). Kenneth Wood's *Atlas for Stamp Collectors* lists local stamps for such odd places as Rattlesnake Island in Lake Erie, Kaulbach Island off the coast

ISLE OF LUNDY 1954

of Nova Scotia, Canada, and Tierra del Fuego. (The latter is divided between Chile and Argentina and the one stamp dates from 1890, when a Romanian gold miner issued it — with a face value of ten centigrams of gold dust — to demonstrate his authority in the Argentinian half of the island.)[2] During the 1970s there was some media interest in the Hutt River Province in Western Australia where a local farming family, following disputes with the government wheat authorities, declared its own state, complete with royal titles, and issued a number of stamps which were bought by tourists despite their total lack of postal validity. In 1988 the New Zealand Government sought a court injunction to prevent a private courier company in the North Island from issuing its own "document exchange stamps".

Postcards, Cancellations and Other Odditiies

In many cases, postal authorities use postcards, special envelopes, postal stationery such as aerograms, and cancellations for various non-postal purposes. A good example is the almost universal issue of "first day covers", specially designed envelopes bearing a stamp cancelled on the day it first went on sale. Some post offices will use specially designed envelopes or cards to commemorate events or anniversaries not deemed worthy of special stamps, and they, too, become objects for collectors. Stamps are often produced in special souvenir sheets by postal authorities. The first "miniature sheet" was issued by Luxembourg in 1923, and since then sheets have often been particularly attractive to collectors. In addition, there are large numbers of seals, stickers, labels, and so on, which resemble stamps, and are often collected — but these fall outside the scope of this book. So, too, do postcards whose invention, apparently in Austria, closely followed that of stamps.

Postmarks, too, provide additional means whereby postal authorities can stamp their messages on envelopes. Examples of propaganda abound, from the tourist promotion of the 1920s — "Come to Sunny Malta, the Island of History and Romance" — to the present, from Britain — "AIDS: Don't die of ignorance".

There have been occasions when the breakdown of normal coin and banknote production has led to stamps being used as substitute currency, and a possible reverse case in Russia during World War I where paper coins have been found used as stamps. More common was the practice of encasing stamps in metal frames and using them as currency, which was done in a number of European countries during and immediately after World War I. Even today stamps are used in lieu of small change in Italy and presumably other countries.

Forgeries and Propaganda

Most forgeries are, naturally, of rare stamps intended for sale to collectors, but there are cases of governments forging stamps of enemy countries. During both World Wars, the German and British governments produced counterfeit copies of each others' stamps so as to distribute war propaganda. The British also produced stamps bearing caricatures of Hitler which were distributed within Germany, while Germany produced British propaganda "stamps" carrying anti-Semitic propaganda. One example has been given of a "stamp" based on the 1935 issue for the Silver Jubilee of George V with Stalin's head replacing that of the King, and with the words, "This War is a Jewish War." [3]

Equally deserving the term forgery are stamps printed for sale to collectors from imaginary countries or countries that have no postal system. Bogus stamps exist for Brunei, issued before there was a postal service in that country and whose only purpose was to extort money from credulous collectors. The most famous example of forgery is the stamps of Moresnet, a non-existent country. In fact the stamps themselves were non-existent; they were conceived and described in a particular European stamp magazine in order to trap other magazines who promptly copied the news — and were thus exposed as plagiarising their information.

1. Advertisement for Jack Koch dealers, *Australian Stamp Monthly*, February 1989, p. 30.
2. K. Wood, *Where in the World?*, Van Dahl Publications, Albany, Oregon, 1983, p. 408.
3. J. Buchan, "Hearts and Minds", *Stamps & Foreign Stamps*, May 1985, p. 6.

C H A P T E R   T H R E E

A CERTAIN PICTURE
OF THE WORLD

*I conceive of a stamp being a fragment of history, a word
in the annals of human experience, a picture of an ideal
fresh from the human heart. The design impressed upon
it signifies what the nation may be at the moment.*
Harold Ickes, former United States Secretary of the
Interior

Raymond Williams has argued that governments use "the
rhetoric of an increasingly superficial and frenetic nationalism as a way of overriding all the real and increasing divisions
and conflicts of interest within what might be the true nation,
the actual and diverse people."[1] He cites as mechanisms used
for these purposes, images such as the monarchy, the "heritage", the armed forces, the flag etc. In their small way, stamps
fit clearly into this framework. Trivial as they may seem, they
are objects that are extremely widely dispersed, both domesti-
cally and abroad and which allow governments to propagate
widely the official culture of a given state.

With the proliferation of new states in the 20th
century — from around 70 to 170 plus since World War II —
comes an emphasis on nationalism and national identity. To

help maintain their control, governments seek to use all means available to bolster a sense of national unity and loyalty to central governments rather than tribes, regions or ethnic and language groups. Stamps are both a part and a reflection of the creation of national consensus, a symbol of governments' determination to maintain control of postal services and to create certain images of the nation, both at home and abroad. For newly independent governments the issuing of stamps is one of the first available acts to proclaim their sovereignty. Equally, changes in name or political status are often first recorded on stamps.

Thus, governments often use stamps to proclaim national unity, to assert their sovereignty over disputed areas or to proclaim state ideology. This is very evident in the early stamps of states that have had to fight to gain independence. The first stamps of Bangladesh, following the successful revolt against Pakistan in 1971, included images of broken chains, massacres, and calls to support the new nation. Few stamps are as honest about their propagandist intent as the series produced by the tiny republic of San Marino in 1943, while it was under fascist domination. These celebrated the

BENIN 1977

power of the press under the inscription "Propaganda Stampa". Stamps proclaiming official government ideology, such as this anti-imperialist issue from Benin (below left), are quite common.

Stamps and State Rivalries

As long as there have been nation states there have been disputes over territory, and stamps become one area where governments can assert their control over disputed areas. Stamps showing maps of disputed territory are easy ways to state nationalist claims. Among the first stamps of independent Ireland were maps that ignored the existence of British rule in Northern Ireland and showed all Ireland as one country.

Assertions of sovereignty over disputed territory have on several occasions led to major incidents between states. Stamps played a part in the little known Gran Chaco War between Bolivia and Paraguay (1932-5), which cost 100,000 lives. The territory had been disputed for many years and tensions mounted in the late 1920s. Moves towards war were hastened by the issue of a Bolivian stamp in 1930 with a map claiming the disputed territory. Two years later, with the outbreak of war, Paraguay retaliated with a series of stamps showing the Chaco and proclaiming "Has been, is and will be". Fighting ended after various international attempts at mediation and gave most of the territory to Paraguay. Not surprisingly, Paraguay (but not Bolivia) issued a series to commemorate the final peace conference and settlement.

ARGENTINA 1936

ARGENTINA 1982

ARGENTINA'S PHILATELIC LAND CLAIMS

Rather than issuing separate stamps for "its" Antarctic territories, Argentina has issued stamps illustrating its claims. One of these issues, in 1964, was paired with a stamp also proclaiming the Falklands (Malvinas) as Argentinian.

Britain annexed the Falklands in 1833, when Captain Onslow landed on the islands and expelled an Argentinian garrison. This annexation has never been recognised by Argentina and from the beginning of this century Argentina sought to have the Universal Postal Union recognise its claim. Thus, when the Falklands issued a series of stamps in 1933 for the centenary of British control, Argentina refused to accept letters bearing the stamps and responded with a stamp in 1936 showing the Falklands as part of Argentinian territory, a stamp that also laid claim to certain Chilean territory and which was withdrawn after pressure from Santiago. The redrawn stamp retained, however, the claim to the Malvinas.

The recent Argentinian invasion of the Falklands was preceded by several Argentinian stamp issues, and the invasion itself was commemorated by special stamps depicting claims to the islands, some of which appeared after the British had reconquered most of the islands. The reconquest was marked by a number of issues from the Falklands reasserting British sovereignty, including two showing the map of the islands which had been used on television news during the war, and which bore a surcharge for post-war rebuilding. When Prince Andrew married Sarah Ferguson in 1986, one of the commemorative stamps from the Falklands showed him wearing the uniform in

FALKLAND ISLANDS 1983

which he had served during the war. Although Britain itself did not commemorate the Falklands War, the interest it engendered has proved a boost for the value of Falklands stamps.[2]

Germany's annexation of various parts of "the homeland" during the late 1930s was the basis for several stamp issues. A 1938 stamp (overleaf) commemorated the "Anschluss" with Austria and also allowed for the assertion of Nazi ideology. (So fast was "Anschluss" that one can find envelopes that used both German and Austrian stamps.) The government of Taiwan sought to keep alive its claim to be the government of all China by issuing stamps showing scenes from Mongolia and Tibet, and Spain has depicted Gibraltar

FALKLAND ISLANDS 1986

GERMANY 1938

on its stamps for similar reasons. Britain issued a set of stamps for Gibraltar in 1968 to mark "Human Rights" — not a common theme for British issues — with the word FREEDOM rising above the rock in a clear propaganda rebuke of Franco's Spain. Spain hit back the following year with stamps to aid those Spanish workers expelled from Gibraltar. In 1985 tensions arose over an Indian stamp showing Jammu and Kashmir, territories also claimed by Pakistan, as part of India. Ironically, the stamp was issued to celebrate a summit conference on "South Asian Regional Co-operation", leading to the cancellation of a ceremony where leaders were to sign first-day covers from each of the seven countries represented. India may well have remembered the 1973 Pakistani stamp that attacked it for its treatment of POWs after the Bangladesh War. West German stamps marking "the integration of Germans driven from their homes" in the Eastern bloc have been refused delivery by East Germany.

Stamps and Foreign Policy

Foreign policy goals, including attacks on other countries, are not infrequently proclaimed on stamps. Such examples are stamps from North Korea proclaiming "Smash Japanese Imperialism" or those campaigning for the withdrawal of US forces. (The stamp top right shows pens belonging to "Anti-US Imperialism Journalists" attacking President Nixon.) Other examples (on page 43) are Egypt's stamp following the Israeli attack on a Libyan airliner in 1973 and Greek stamps in support of union with Cyprus in 1954, which showed pages from the British Hansard covered with an ink blot. Greece subsequently prepared a stamp showing a portrait of Archbi-

GIBRALTAR 1968

NORTH KOREA 1969

NORTH KOREA 1969

EGYPT 1973

GREECE 1954

shop Makarios, whom the British had expelled from Cyprus, and a quotation from Winston Churchill, when Home Secretary in 1905, in support of Cypriot union with Greece. Considerable pressure from Britain prevented the stamp being issued.[3] Most Islamic countries, in recent years, have produced stamps in support of the Palestinians, and an increasing number of stamps have been issued showing support for the anti-apartheid struggle and the independence of South African ruled Namibia (South West Africa). Pakistan has made support for Afghani refugees a theme of recent stamps.

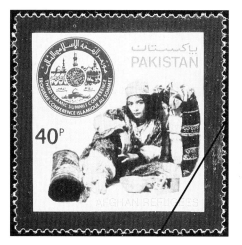

PAKISTAN 1981

In the 1980s the most constant expressions of such propaganda have come from Iran, which has produced considerable numbers of stamps illustrating its battles with the United States, with Iraq and with the moderate Arab states, as well as other stamps supporting Palestinian and Afghan uprisings. Combined with annual issues commemorating the anniversaries of the Shah's overthrow and other issues of religious significance, they give Iranian stamps a peculiarly distinctive flavour. It is one of the very few countries that seems unwilling to compromise its stamp designs in order to attract the western stamp collector.

Stamps can equally be used to show friendship between states and there is an increasing number of joint issues to show good relations between two or more states. The United States has a long history of stamps demonstrating its friendship with other countries. In recent years it has produced joint stamp issues with, among others, Sweden, the Netherlands, Morocco, Australia and France. The opening of the joint Romanian-Yugoslav Iron Gate dam on the Danube in 1965 led to a common stamp issue bearing the value in both currencies — the only example to date of one stamp being valid in two independent countries. However, since 1956, most of the countries of Western Europe have issued stamps in honour of "Europa", often with common designs.

IRAN 1980s

DOMINICA 1976; POLAND 1972

NICARAGUA 1974

Large numbers of countries have issued stamps to commemorate the bicentenaries of the American and French Revolutions, the fiftieth anniversary of the USSR, and the deaths or anniversaries of political figures such as Lenin, Churchill, Bolivar and John F. Kennedy. Without access to a computer program, it is impossible to say whose portraits have appeared most often on stamps. Other than British Royals, I suspect the list would include those mentioned above, plus Rowland Hill, Napoleon, Christopher Columbus and possibly Karl Marx, who first appeared on a stamp in 1919 during the short-lived Soviet Republic of Hungary. Most African countries have issued stamps in honour of Martin Luther King, and Liberia, particularly attentive to American collectors, has honoured every American President, including George Bush (who cannot appear on a US stamp while he is still alive).

PARAGUAY 1966

POLAND 1937

One of the earliest national celebrations to be taken up by large numbers of countries was the 150th anniversary of the ratification of the United States Constitution, which was marked by stamps from 15 countries, including China, France, Turkey and many Latin American states. One catalogue of the time proclaimed that, "It appears that no expense was too great, no time too long and no effort too much for these nations to show their regard for the United States in preparing postage stamps having the magnificence of the Constitution Series."[4] Of course, this was nothing beside the number of countries that marked the Bicentenary of the American Revolution in 1976. Even Britain decided on a stamp for the event with a portrait of Benjamin Franklin, a primary negotiator of the final peace treaty with Britain. This was despite some official fears that, "However it might be approached in design terms, there would be a danger that ordinary people would criticise the issue as celebrating a defeat. Moreover there could well be feeling in those former British colonies which achieved independence later and without bloodshed that... we should seem to honour those who rebelled."[5] The Australian Bicentenary saw joint stamp issues with Britain, the United States (see right) and New Zealand, as well as issues from Israel, Ireland, the Netherlands and some Pacific islands. And the year 1989 saw a proliferation of issues for the bicentenary of the French Revolution.

The commemoration of foreign nationals or events can be used to great effect by countries to emphasise their foreign policy. Thus India has demonstrated both its nonalignment and its international standing by issuing stamps to commemorate both Marx and Franklin Roosevelt in the same year. In the 1950s, as part of the Cold War rhetoric of the time, the United States issued a series of stamps commemorating "champions of liberty", showing both US allies (President

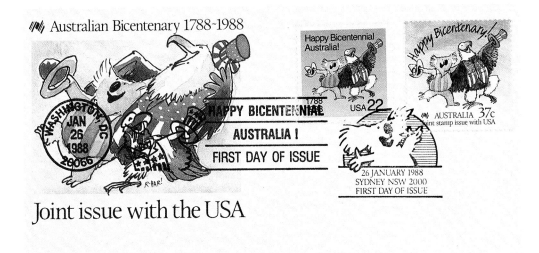

Joint issue with the USA

AUSTRALIA; UNITED STATES OF AMERICA 1988

Magsaysay of the Philippines) and anti-communist martyrs (such as Thomas Masaryk from Czechoslovakia). Czechoslovakia underlined its dependence on the USSR when, in 1983, it honoured Soviet military commanders on stamps and the countries of the Eastern Bloc have been particularly fond of stamps proclaiming "solidarity" and "friendship". In the commemorative issue for the 25th anniversary of the death of John Kennedy the administration of the Marshall Islands, a US protectorate, decided on a piece of highly charged propaganda by showing nuclear tests off the Bikini Atoll inscribed "Diminishing the Nuclear Threat".

There are very few countries that have not depicted foreign nationals on their stamps. Sweden, for example, has gradually been portraying all Nobel Prize winners and South Korea has regularly inscribed on stamps every visiting head of state. Stamps provide a cheap and visible way of paying tribute to foreign governments and of legitimising one's own, as in the example of the Korean stamps.

NICARAGUA AND THE UNITED STATES

In March 1985, as part of the US administration's campaign against Nicaragua, Vice-President Bush brandished several stamps bearing portraits of Karl Marx to "prove" that the Sandanista government were really Marxists. He neglected to point out that the current government had also issued stamps showing George Washington and Pope John Paul II.

The use of stamps to "prove" a case against Nicaragua is not particular to the present. In 1901, during a Senate debate on whether to cut a canal from the Atlantic to the Pacific through Nicaragua or Panama, Senator Mark Hanna mailed a Nicaraguan stamp to all Senators. It showed the Motombo volcano "in glorious eruption", thus reinforcing Hanna's argument against building the canal in Nicaragua. In 1937 a stamp showing a map of Nicaragua with an incorrect boundary almost provoked a war with Honduras, whose territory had been encroached upon.

Nicaraguan stamps offer a running commentary on the history of that country. There is evidence of the very strong American influence, with stamps commemorating the actor Will Rogers and his role in earthquake relief, Cardinal Spellman and, frequently, baseball. The long reign of the dictator Somoza is marked by stamps proclaiming his commitment to democracy and world peace through appearances alongside Franklin Roosevelt, UN Secretary General U. Thant and John Kennedy, and by stamps designed for the American stamp market, with issues showing opera singers and fictional detectives. The triumph of the Sandanistas was commemorated in a number of stamps, even as they continue to produce issues designed to be bought by the school children of the world (see page 49).

NICARAGUA
1939; 1948; 1964

NICARAGUA 1980s

Peace and War

As will already be obvious, stamps often illustrate war, both in terms of design and changes in sovereignty. Occupying forces quickly issue stamps to mark their control, even if they are no more than overprints on already existing stamps, and there are a number of stamps produced for the exclusive use of the armed forces. The need for extra revenue in war time produces a fair number of "war tax" stamps. These were pioneered by Spain as far back as 1874 and taken up by several Australian states during the Boer War. Surcharges for various war causes were common during World War I — war tax stamps were compulsory in Canada — and as one observer wrote tartly, "It is kinder to suppose that the frequent changes in these war tax stamps, particularly in some British colonies, were the result of uncertainty as to how long the war taxes were to endure, than to suggest that an attack was being made on the purses of collectors, who at that time were interested in war stamps and very little else."[6] The end of both World Wars produced a number of peace, and sometimes victory, stamps as well as changes in the issuing authorities. Following Germany's defeat in 1945, a number of different issues appeared in the various occupied zones, with France, in particular, producing stamps for each of the German states under its control.

Stamps are used, too, as part of the total war effort, both as morale boosters and as devices to raise funds for war charities. During World War II, the Soviet Union issued large numbers of stamps showing aspects of the war effort — Soviet victories, war heroes, scenes of battles and war medals. Japan charted some of its war gains with stamps marking the surrender of Singapore and the attack on Pearl Harbor. Not surprisingly, its last war stamp came in 1942, the high point of its conquests. During the course of the Korean War, the North commemorated its capture of Seoul, while the South underlined international support with a series showing the flags of each of the 21 nations who contributed troops to United Nations forces in the war.

USSR 1944

One can chart some of the progress of the Vietnam War via the stamps of the two Vietnams, plus some of their allies. During the war against the French that followed their return to Indo-China after the Japanese defeat in World War II, the Vietnamese independence movement, under Ho Chi Minh, produced its own stamps, some expressed in terms of weights of rice. After the Geneva Conference of 1954 divided the country into two, Communist rebels in the South received increasing aid from the North, while the United States became more and more embroiled in propping up the government of the South. Both South and North issued large numbers of stamps marking the progress of the war, with themes such as "Free World's Aid to Vietnam" versus "1,000th US Aircraft Brought Down over Vietnam". From 1963 on, the National Liberation Front

**NATIONAL LIBERATION
FRONT OF VIETNAM 1965**

issued its own stamps for use in those areas of the South they controlled, almost all of them with explicitly political themes. The propaganda uses of these stamps were underlined by the fact that the first issue in 1963 came with inscriptions in English, French and Spanish. The end of fighting in 1975 saw the creation of one Socialist Republic of Vietnam, which, like other Communist states, combines political propaganda and appeal to collectors in its stamp issuing policy.

Sometimes one learns more from what might have been. I have been shown advertisements in an American stamp magazine for "tragic unissued stamps of South Vietnam", including issues for "the Planned Invasion of North Vietnam that never came", and for a Buddhist set "prepared but never released due to the Buddhist anti-government demonstration".

While both Vietnams issued large numbers of stamps showing the progress of the war, other combatant countries were far less assertive. Despite the enormous commitment of United States military to the war, it went unmarked by the US Post Office until 1979 — four years after the final troop withdrawal — when there was an issue honouring Vietnam veterans and a later one for the Vietnam Memorial in Washington. Of the other countries whose troops supported the South, only South Korea has so far recognised the war on its stamps. Participation in the war was obviously too controversial for stamps from Australia, New Zealand or the Philippines, just as France had lost a bloody war 20 years earlier without marking it on stamps. The North's allies were less forbearing, with East Germany and Cuba particularly assiduous in expressing support for the North (see above right).

**CUBA 1964;
EAST GERMANY 1968, 1979**

USSR 1984; CANADA 1986

Some countries have used stamps to promote the idea of peace and co-operation. The first peace propaganda stamps were probably those issued by Switzerland to mark the end of World War I. Since World War II, the Soviets have been particularly attached to stamps promoting these themes, but the International Year of Peace (1986) saw a large number of states produce stamps with this theme. It would be unfair to read too much into the fact that the United States was not one of them as the United States does not generally honour "International Years" on its stamps. In 1975, perhaps only coincidentally the year of its retreat from Vietnam, it did issue a stamp proclaiming "World peace through law".

Stamps and State Ideology

Stamps with explicitly political messages are not uncommon, even though the intensely conservative stamp-collecting world chooses to ignore this. There are a number of stamps that act as political posters in miniature, serving to spell out the official creed of the state. These are often explicit, such as Libyan stamps depicting Colonel Ghadaffi and his Green Book, or American stamps proclaiming the text of the Declaration of Independence, but ideological evangelising underlies a whole range of stamp issues.

The United States, along with China under Mao, stands out for the number of stamps proclaiming its official ideology. Franklin Roosevelt took a personal interest in US stamps and used them early on in his Administration to commemorate at least one aspect of the "New Deal", namely the National Recovery Act, but the memorialisation of the American creed goes back to the first portraits of Washington and Franklin and stamps showing the signing of the Declaration of Independence in 1869. Over the past few decades, American stamps have frequently carried the texts of classic American liberalism, including patriotic sayings from the Founding Fathers and slogans such as, "To cast a free ballot is the root of democracy", and, "The people's right to petition for redress".

UNITED STATES OF AMERICA 1986; 1974; 1975

Such ideological issues were more than balanced by China in the 1960s, with issues in strident red and gold, which included the text of Chairman Mao's "Anti-American declaration" and some of his poems. Between 1966 and 1969 no fewer than 70 stamps were issued showing either Mao or the words of Mao, which may well be a record for philatelic

CHINA 1972

hagiolatry. Recent Chinese stamps have been noticeably less overtly political in their messages.

Few authoritarian rulers have used stamps to cement their role to this extent. Hitler appeared for the first time on a stamp in 1938 marking his birthday, which became an annual issue, and was also commemorated on stamps issued by German puppet governments in Bohemia and Poland. Other puppet governments were encouraged to promote their own nationalism, so that stamps issued by pro-Nazi governments in Croatia (part of Yugoslavia) and Slovakia (part of Czechoslovakia) show, not Hitler, but local fascist heroes and insignia.

Nazi German stamps presented a sanitised vision of life under the Third Reich and were less propagandistic than one might expect — some of the propaganda is discussed in the section on design. There were some stamps showing Nazi victories and insignia, but no reference to concentration camps, anti-semitism, or the eradication of all

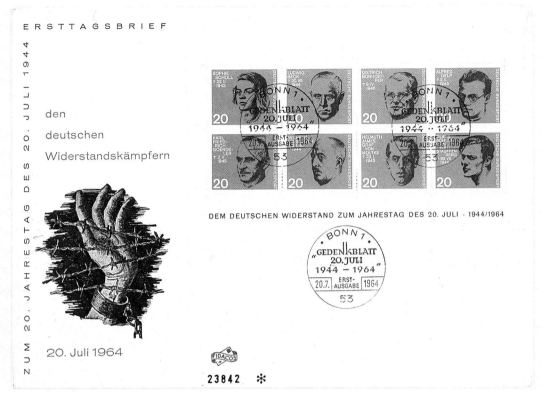

WEST GERMANY 1964

AUSTRIA 1946

opposition. Only well into the War do a lot of stamps have military themes. East Germany issued a number of stamps since World War II showing the evils of Nazi rule — concentration camps and their victims — as well as Germans who resisted. West Germany took longer to do so. The first anti-Nazi stamp came in 1964, commemorating the 20th anniversary of the attempt on Hitler's life (previous page). Austria, however, wasted no time. Its series for the 1946 anti-fascist Exhibition carefully portrayed Austria as the victim, rather than in any way the collaborator, of Nazism (previous page). Unlike both Germanies, subsequent stamp-issuing policy seems to be to ignore the whole question, a reflection of general Austrian attitudes.

The only Italian stamps to bear Mussolini's portrait marked Italo-German friendship, and showed him alongside Hitler. (Italy, of course, remained a monarchy through the fascist period and portrayed its King on some stamps.) Stalin first appeared on a Russian stamp in 1934 to mark the tenth anniversary of the death of Lenin, but on remarkably few subsequent issues. Only Albania and China honoured his birth centenary in 1979. More contemporary rulers — Bokassa in the Central African Republic, Nkrumah in Ghana, Soeharto in Indonesia, Marcos in the Philippines — have been less self-abnegating.

As well as proclaiming official ideology, stamps can be used to legitimise constitutional change or unpopular governments, as in the stamp issued by the Philippines under Marcos that proclaimed his support for "tenant emancipation", or the issue during the period of military government of Brazil for "human rights". But not only authoritarian governments proclaim official ideology via stamps. An uncomfortable reminder of this comes from Australia, whose

PAKISTAN 1984

first issue showed a kangaroo superimposed on a map of Australia. The Postmaster General of the time, Mr Frazer (Labor), later stated that the map was white to make clear Australia's policy in regard to its population, which was then based on the total exclusion of anyone of non-European origin.[7]

The most common way in which stamps reflect official ideology is in their depiction of a country's history. Stamps bear out very clearly the maxim that history is the tale written by the victors.

Stamps and the Commemoration of History

A number of countries have sought to commemorate aspects of their history on stamps. In the 1920s Portugal produced a number of series depicting highlights of the national history. The official version of a country's history has rarely been as clearly set out as on a series of French stamps issued between 1966 and 1973. They portray a pictorial history of France, from the rebellion of the Gauls against Rome under the leadership of Vercingetorix, until the rise of Napoleon, when the series ended. Obviously a great deal of careful selection was involved. One stamp marked the Edict of Nantes, which extended toleration to Protestants, but not the massacre of St Bartholomew's Day which preceded it. The Revolution received several issues, but there was no reference to the execution of the King, nor the Reign of Terror. That Napoleon appeared on three stamps may be due to the fact that the stamps were issued by Gaullist governments who might be expected to venerate Napoleon more than governments of the

FRANCE 1968; 1970

left. Of course, no French defeat was included. The loss of Quebec, or Waterloo, was not considered appropriate for commemoration.

Even so, it takes a considerable sense of national purpose to be able to produce a series commemorating 19 centuries of continuous history. Few countries have anything like a continuous history for such a long period, without major periods of foreign conquest and occupation. Probably only Britain, Japan and China could attempt a similar series, and in all three cases there are certain historical problems. A plan of Tony Benn's to issue stamps showing all British rulers since William the Conqueror was shelved, partly because of the incongruity of showing the Lord Protector, Oliver Cromwell, alongside an effigy of the Queen, whose ancestor, Charles I, was executed by Cromwell's forces. Japan, probably as part of its national insecurity after World War II, very rarely issues stamps with historical references.

The French series is an example on a large scale of the common belief that commemorating history is a way of saying something about the official definition of the present. Compare the French historical set with the 1986 stamp — issued by a Socialist government — commemorating the Popular Front government of Socialists and Communists of 1936, or the success of Tony Benn in issuing stamps to honour Ghandi and the free-thinking Scottish poet, Robert Burns. Like France, the United States issues large numbers of stamps referring to its history, usually post-Independence — and here, too, there's something of a shift in recent years. The 1976 stamps for the Bicentenary of the American Revolution deliberately sought to include "the common people", with stamps showing, as "contributors to the cause", two enlisted men (Peter Francisco and Salem Poor), a Jewish financier, Hyam Salomen, and a Connecticut woman, Sybil Ludington.[8]

FRANCE 1986

In the past century almost every revolution, civil war or change of regime has meant new images on stamps, as governments seek to bring symbols into line with ideology. Thus Chile under Allende issued stamps commemorating the takeover of the coppermines, while under Pinochet it has honoured the military. The various shifts in government in Peru over the past two decades are reflected in stamps hailing the "unity of the armed forces and people" (in 1970) and "the return to democracy" (1980). The revolution that brought Colonel Ghadaffi to power in Libya in 1969 is commemorated each year with special stamps, usually bearing images of military or economic might.

CHILE 1984

One of the best examples in shifting imagery comes from Spain (page 60), with the last issues of the Republican government (in 1938) showing militia defending their territory — there was a special overprint to commemorate the defence of Madrid — while Franco's Nationalists, who first issued stamps in 1936, almost three years before their final victory, appealed to religious symbols such as Isabella the Catholic and the Holy Year of Compostella. General Franco himself first appeared on a series of definitive stamps in 1939.

SPAIN 1938

Political changes meant clear shifts in the design of Italian stamps after Mussolini's accession to power, and in designs in the Soviet Union, in Cuba, in Iran (where an overprint covered the Shah's portrait before new stamps could be designed and issued) and in China. The history of Chinese stamps was complicated by the Japanese occupation and by the existence of temporary local governments under Communist control. In 1949, stamps were issued by the Nationalist government of Chiang-kai-Shek, by provincial governments (the Gibbons catalogue lists eight areas) and by the victorious Communist government. The official explanation of the military takeover in Indonesia in 1965 was underlined by a series of stamps commemorating "victims" (all military figures) "of the attempted Communist coup".

USSR 1917; 1921

The short-lived local autonomy of a number of areas after the Russian Revolution has already been mentioned. In 1917, two stamps celebrated the overthrow of the Czar, but the first Soviet stamps only appeared in 1921, three years after the Communist Party had taken power, and showed symbols of agriculture, industry, science and arts. Definitive stamps showing workers, soldiers and peasants soon followed, and have remained staples of Soviet definitives.

Nor are such changes confined to the dramatic changes in regime. One can see a clear shift in what is seen as worthy of commemoration on British stamps between the period of Labour government in the 1960s, when Tony Benn was Postmaster General, and the Thatcherite 1980s. Compare 1968 — when anniversaries commemorated included the Trade Union Congress and suffragette Emmeline Pankhurst — with issues 20 years later. British stamps for 1988 included commemoration of the defeat of the Spanish Armada, the Welsh Bible and, although Benn presumably would approve of these stamps, the anniversary of poet Edward Lear. The nostalgia for a mythical and stable national past, which has been identified as part of the appeal of Margaret Thatcher,[9] appears in recent stamps commemorating the Arthurian legend, heraldic orders and Victorian England. Even where there are attempts to prevent stamps from being too politicised, postal authorities, in the words once used by the US Supreme Court, follow the election returns.

Tony Benn spoke of the celebratory role of stamps, and while he included certain radical achievements in his version of what should be celebrated (boasting of the black face that appeared on the stamp for the Salvation Army and of the issue honouring Robert Burns, who was both an atheist and a republican) few of his counterparts have risked such potentially controversial issues. More common is the blandness that typifies both the stamps of the United States and the Soviet Union, whose issues are clear examples of national self-congratulation.

Thus stamps become means of celebrating national achievement, whether in space, sport or culture. Increasingly, the scope of such achievement broadens, with popular and folk arts now common themes for stamp issues. As stamps have become less pompous, there is room for

USSR 1961

GREAT BRITAIN 1988

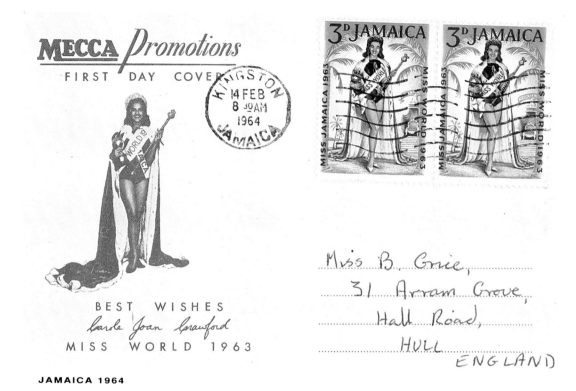

celebration of all sorts, and there are several stamps commemorating the winning of a Miss World title, the world heavyweight boxing title fight between Muhammad Ali and George Foreman in Zaire in 1974, and the World Rubik Cube championship in Hungary in 1982. For many countries a commemorative stamp has become a standard way to honour a particular individual, whether it be the Colombian writer Gabriel Marquez winning the Nobel Prize for Literature, or the Tanzanian runner Filbert Bayi winning a gold medal at the Montreal Olympics. Some countries on the other hand have a firm ban on the depiction of any living person other than the sovereign on their stamps.

Defining National Identity

Most governments have turned to symbolic representation of the nation for stamp designs, whether these be the various stylised female heads that have been used by France, or the shells used by Pacific states such as Papua New Guinea or Aitutaki. In some cases, such as Australia, one can see the search for national symbols reflected on stamps.

The first Australian federal issue in 1913 — stamps from the six colonies were used for the previous 12 years following federation — showed a kangaroo astride a map of Australia. A change in government from Labor, which was far less supportive of the Imperial ties, to the conservative Liberal Party, saw these supplemented by a series bearing the portrait of George V. The same ambivalence between national and Imperial themes has persisted until the present. Under the conservative Liberal government of Malcolm Fraser, an annual issue for Australia Day was inaugurated in 1978, followed by one for the Queen's birthday two years later.

AUSTRALIA 1913; 1914

AUSTRALIA 1934

AUSTRALIA 1985

Aborigines have been featured on more and more Australian stamps as governments attempt to incorporate them into the hitherto totally European conception of Australian identity. An Aboriginal figure first appeared on a 1934 stamp for the Victorian centenary, depicted as a wild native gazing at the modern city of Melbourne (page 63). Aboriginal art and figures began to be used in stamp design after 1948. In 1968 the artist Namatjira was included in a series of "famous Australians", and in 1975, the last full-blood Tasmanian, Truganini, appeared in a series honouring Australian women. In 1982 the Australia Day issue showed the image of Captain Phillip, commander of the First Fleet, alongside an obviously non-Anglo-Saxon immigrant and an Aborigine. Aboriginal art appeared on several stamps, including the one commemorating the opening of the National Gallery in Canberra, and was the theme of a series of stamps issued in 1985, the first in the lead up to the Bicentenary of British settlement in 1988.

The final set, in what was a total of 47 stamps culminating in Australia Day 1988, is symbolic of how Australian history has been understood by dominant white culture. The Aborigines who appear on the first two stamps of the strip have been totally replaced by British soldiers and sailors in the final stamp.

AUSTRALIA 1988

*One does see, however, some hint in the last but
one stamp of Aboriginal resistance, as had been true in one
of the strip of stamps issued for the Cook Bicentenary in
1970, where a couple of Aborigines are depicted brandishing
spears as Cook's party lands at Botany Bay.*[10]

Where conflict over language reflects larger conflicts over national identity, the question is immediately posed
of which language to use on stamps. Canada, South Africa
and Belgium carefully balance their two official languages
and, in the case of Canada, there is great care to give equal
recognition to both French and English speakers in those
honoured on stamps. For a time, South Africa issued both an
English and an Afrikaans version of each stamp, although
since 1967 it uses the bilingual abbreviation RSA to identify its
stamps. Norway — which recognises two versions of its language — alternates between "Noreg" and "Norge" to identify
its issues, while Ireland fluctuates between use of Gaelic and
English. India uses both English and Hindi on its stamps and
the Philippines sometimes uses English and sometimes
Tagalog in identifying the subject of stamps. The Swiss use
the Latin name Helvetia to avoid the whole problem — and
identify their youth charity stamps as "Pro Juvente".

As the Australian case suggests, "settler societies",
that is, those countries established as part of the great expansion of Europe into the rest of the world over the past few
centuries, pose particular problems for stamp designers, in
that the great events and victories of European settlement also
mark the defeat and often partial genocide of the original
inhabitants. Solutions to this dilemma range from New Zealand's, which has long been to recognise Maori culture and
history on its stamps (showing a Maori canoe as far back as

NEW ZEALAND 1985

CANADA 1972

1898) to South Africa's position, which has yet to depict a non-white on its stamps.

Since the 1930s the history of the Boers, and above all their "Great Trek" into the inland of the country, has been a prominent feature of South African stamps. After all, the policy of apartheid is reflected in "black only" faces on stamps from the "homelands". So far the Soviet Union has rarely acknowledged non-Russian culture on its stamps — and ignored the diversity of languages spoken in the USSR. The United States in recent years has stressed ethnic diversity, but has paid less attention to its indigenous peoples than Canada, which has issued a number of stamps showing Indian and Inuit culture, or New Zealand.

Most interesting in this regard are those countries of Central and South America with a strong Indian heritage, which is rarely reflected on their stamps. Peru, for example, whose current population is about half Indian, barely acknowledged its rich indigenous history for the first 100 years of its postal history, preferring to honour Spaniards such as Pizarro, the independence movement of Simon Bolivar and Catholic saints. More recently, especially with nationalist governments, Peruvian authorities have produced a number of stamps showing aspects of Incan culture. Other countries with a large Indian population, such as Bolivia and Paraguay, have issued similar stamps, although they are more likely to depict European art than their own culture, and their stamp designs are strongly Eurocentric. Mexico has done slightly better, with acknowledgements of its Aztec past on stamps since the 1930s.

Even in Europe, the same stress on the official definition of a cultural identity that denies ethnic hetero-geneity is common. I know of no stamps showing gypsies, for

PARAGUAY 1970; PERU 1972; MEXICO 1934

example. Greek stamps reflect a larger phenomenon, namely the creation of a definition of modern Greece as the direct descendant of ancient Hellas and the repudiation of the influence of centuries of Ottoman rule. The very heavy emphasis on classical themes on Greek stamps, from the earliest issues to the present, is explained in these comments from a book on critical ethnography: "Throughout the [19th] century interested European classicists, and men of letters generally, tutored the Greeks in constructing a Hellenic image which all could accept as worthy of the nation which had first given light to the West. This entailed suppressing, if not eradicating, all traces of Greece's more recently acquired Oriental culture, its so-called *Romiossini*. The language, for example, was purged of Turkish features and modelled on ancient Greek, and Ottoman-period houses were progressively torn down and replaced with neo-classical structures."[11]

GREECE 1983; 1942; 1911

ISRAEL 1980

ISRAEL 1976

The clearest case of using stamps to define the national identity may well come from Israel, which has consciously used stamps through its 40-year history to emphasise the official definition of itself as a Jewish state. Israeli stamps, while including themes such as landscapes and animals, have tended to be heavily oriented towards nation building, and to the depiction of Jewish history, from Biblical references to Noah's Ark and the flight from Egypt, through the history of the Diaspora, the foundation of Israel, and subsequent disputes over territory. The non-Jewish population of Israel is never acknowledged, and non-Jews appear on Israeli stamps only when there is a clear link to Jewish history.

The market for Israeli stamps among collectors is not unimportant, but this is probably a secondary consideration beside the quite systematic use of stamps to develop a particular national identity, and to stress the Jewishness of the Israeli state. This is furthered by the distinctive design of Israeli stamps (often unusually long and thin, and all bearing a descriptive "tab" at the bottom of each sheet of stamps), and by the more recent emphasis on military themes.

Internationalism

In different ways, governments use stamps to show their allegiance to internationalism and universal values. Raymond Williams has pointed to the apparent paradox that modern states promote both nationalism and internationalism at the same time and for similar reasons. As governments produce stamps stressing national accomplishments and identity, they also promote certain internationalist values, such as peace, co-operation and friendship. Even Israel, which is far less inclined to such themes than most, issued stamps for the Montreal Olympics and the International Year of the Child.

One of the clichés about stamp collecting is that it promotes international understanding and harmony. The Secretary General of the United Nations, Perez de Cuellar, claimed that, "Stamps carry a message of their own and lead to world understanding."[12] More accurately, their message is likely to reflect the dominant international rhetoric of the time, and is as likely to obscure as to promote understanding. The stamps issued by the United Nations for use at their offices in New York, Geneva and Vienna, are the closest guide to the current language of political piety we possess. In addition to commemorating specific UN agencies and programs, recent issues have espoused such issues as conservation, human rights and opposition to racism. Other issues are somewhat more contentious, such as stamps proclaiming the new international economic order or the rights of the Palestinians, but again they reflect the dominant international language.

This language is reflected in the declaration of international years and common stamp issues. Some countries are particularly fond of the former, such as Kuwait, which in 1983 found six "international days" to commemorate, including world health, environment and the International Maritime Organisation. Thailand has produced an annual issue for United Nations Day since 1951, and even an isolated country such as Burma — which in recent years has issued fewer stamps than almost any other country — has tended to show its allegiance to international years. There are a large number of stamps recognising the work of international

UNITED NATIONS
(peace) 1961;
(education) 1964

THAILAND 1974;
INDONESIA 1970

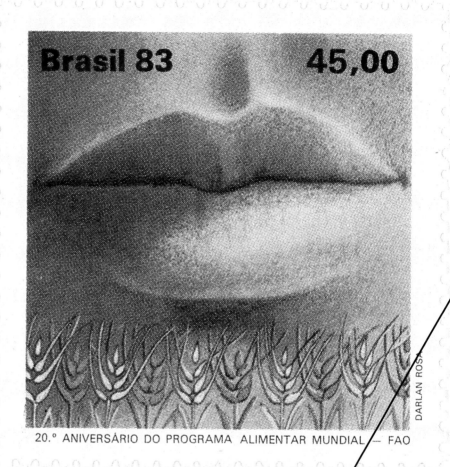

BRAZIL 1983

organisations, such as this one from Brazil (left) commemorating the World Food Project of the Food and Agricultural Organisation. These issues may be less cynical than appears, for the reality is that many international agencies are more significant for Third World than First World nations.

It is instructive to look at how different countries commemorate "international years". During the International Year of Women in 1975 large numbers of countries produced stamps for this year, including a number whose commitment to equality for women was, at least, questionable — Paraguay and Pakistan, for example — but very few recognised through their stamps the existence of a women's movement, or any conception of women's oppression. The most common designs used symbols, sometimes very indirect. The Netherlands showed a playing card with the heads of a woman and man, while Norway showed the image of three women on a wrought iron gate. Some countries issued stamps showing well-known women (Liberia managed to include both Joan of Arc and American singer Mahalia Jackson), while a number of governments took advantage of the year for their own ideological purposes: the Philippines pictured Imelda Marcos, well-coiffeured, beside the IWY (International Women's Year) emblem. Sometimes women's concerns were linked to government commitment to economic development, as in this stamp from Ghana. Strikingly, hardly any stamps recognised women who had specifically fought for women's rights. Feminism, as distinct from an official interpretation of IWY, went almost unrecognised.

ITALY 1975

GHANA 1975

TONGA 1978

There are real problems in "reading" the commitment to international themes on stamps. In recent years, conservation themes have become quite prominent on stamps, with all sorts of countries promoting their commitment to saving vanishing species, to conserving the environment and to protecting the forests. Sometimes these stamps may represent a genuine concern of the issuing government. But it is also true that it is very easy to issue a stamp — certainly a lot easier than saving a rain forest. The growth of such themes on stamps tells us nothing, in other words, about the realities of government policies, although they may tell us something about the lip-service governments feel obliged to pay to certain international concerns, perhaps as a way of disguising their own inaction. There is a sad irony in the juxtaposition of two Brazilian issues in 1988, one for "protected animals" and one for the National Confederation of Industry.

Common themes are a way of showing international solidarity, as in the stamps produced annually for more than 30 years by the countries of Western Europe to mark their dedication to the idea of European community. These originally shared a common design, but now have separate designs around common themes. Such issues were at first restricted to the six founding members of the European Economic Community, but by the 1980s such "outriders" as Malta, Cyprus and Iceland also issued "European" stamps. Solidarity, too, is displayed in stamps commemorating certain events, whether these be Imperial anniversaries or, as is now more common, stamps supporting the international effort to "save Venice" or the Olympic Games.

Quadrennial issues for the Olympics have become among the most common of all philatelic themes. Greece began the trend in 1896 although it was not until 1920, and the Antwerp Games, that another host country thought the event worthy of commemoration. Today, of course, host countries issue multiple sets, and since the Rome Olympics in 1960, the Games are the occasion for virtually every country in the world to issue a stamp. The ideology of sport as a form of international co-operation is a powerful one in many stamp issues and is also found in the numerous stamps celebrating World Cup football.

Olympic issues can be used simultaneously to promote national and international achievement. As far back as 1924, Uruguay produced stamps to commemorate its football victory at the Paris Olympics. They promote a view of sport as a form of international harmony and peaceful competition that fits quite divergent official ideologies. Sport can both glorify individual and team achievement, while allowing for patriotic displays that have political advantages for incumbent governments, as Ronald Reagan found when the Los Angeles Games coincided with the 1984 election campaign. What other event can be so uniformly hailed and so clearly reveal the convergence of official ideologies? The Moscow Games of 1980 and the Seoul Games of 1988 were both arenas for the depiction of national grandeur. As Ian Buruma wrote in a savage analysis of the 1988 Games, "Communist countries are the most successful Olympic contenders and the true heirs of Coubertin's ideals of Patriotism, Peace and International Brotherhood. In this, as in so many other ways, Communists are the last Victorians."[13] Little wonder that Eastern bloc countries have been fond of stamps depicting official sports contests.

LAOS 1988;
UNITED STATES OF AMERICA 1980;
MEXICO 1968;
GREECE 1984;
USSR 1980

REPUBLIC OF THE CONGO 1966

One sees in a stamp from the Congo an excellent example of the ideology of sport as promoting international harmony (see left). "Sport unites all peoples" says the caption, but "peoples" are depicted entirely as male, and the stamp displays an image of conventional masculinity that is very common on stamps.

The Olympic Games are the best example of how non-government international organisations are taken up on stamps and legitimised. Equally, one could point to the large number of issues for the Red Cross, for Scouts and Guides, for Rotary and the Lions clubs. All these can be seen as examples of the internationalisation of Western values and organisations, and hence part of the construction of a global culture that is depicted on stamps.

As there are more and more stamps produced, they come increasingly to resemble each other. The illustrations of Olympic stamps make the point. Except perhaps for the Greek one, the designs and countries are interchangeable. When traditional European art appears on the stamps of Rwanda and Mali, when Caribbean island states depict classic racing cars and Mongolia issues stamps showing scenes from European operas and Disney cartoons, it is hard to talk of any distinctive national identity being portrayed by stamps. In fact, it becomes necessary to distinguish those stamps aimed primarily at foreign collectors and those aimed at national image making. North Korea's issue of two stamps to commemorate the wedding of Prince Charles and Lady Diana was clearly in the first category (page 76). It was probably impossible to buy the stamps in North Korea at all. They would have gone straight from the printer in Paris to the stamp shops of the First World — one wonders what would have happened to a citizen of Pyongyang bold enough to request the stamp.

**BRAZIL 1977;
WEST GERMANY 1987**

NORTH KOREA 1981

Nonetheless, one can see in the sorts of themes that dominate stamp issues in the present epoch the development of an international culture, one in which certain sorts of activities and events are recognised as worth commemoration, irrespective of national boundaries and official ideologies. Some of the stamps issued to promote conservation and the environment may well be aimed primarily at foreign collectors. At the same time, their popularity over the past decade is a reflection of a growing international awareness, which in time may force governments to act in accordance with their rhetoric.

While most countries will use stamps to commemorate their national cultural heritage, only a certain sort of art is taken up universally — and this is almost invariably what has been defined in the West as "high culture". Shakespeare, Beethoven and Picasso appear very frequently on stamps, as in this scene from Shakespeare's *Midsummer Night's Dream*, but composers or writers from non-Western cultures will rarely be honoured outside their own countries. Thus art on stamps becomes illustrative of the simultaneous phenomena of national and international culture, with most countries showing both their own folk art and also certain accepted masterpieces of the Western canon (page 78). The Soviet Union has been particularly fond of showing its internationalism through stamps honouring the cultural figures of other nations. Even during the height of the Cold War, Soviet stamps celebrated Americans such as the writers Longfellow and Mark Twain.

YUGOSLAVIA 1955

Stamps as Propaganda — Modernisation and Progress

Stamps themselves are symbols of modernisation, so a four-coloured multigravured stamp can be issued by the poorest of countries as a symbol that it, too, is part of the modern world. Little wonder that "modernisation" is one of the most frequent themes of stamps from "developing" countries.

One of the central tenets of almost all national ideologies is that of progress, which is usually equated with growth, development and industrialisation. As Donald Horne put it, "In this respect the Soviet Union and the United States, Japan and France, Bulgaria and Australia can be seen, in overall outline, as the same: in all of them, capital surpluses are accumulated centrally for investment and, in all of them, humans are "normalised" to fit into "working life".[14]

RWANDA 1971

EQUATORIAL GUINEA 1973

PAPUA NEW GUINEA 1964

CHINA 1953

Thus airports and steel mills are common themes on stamps, and most Third World countries are more likely to commemorate economic development on their stamps than to depict their pre-colonial past. Whether it be Turkey honouring industrialisation under Ataturk, Nauru commemorating the phosphate industry, or South Korea vaunting its car production, the stress on industry, growth and exports is universal (see page 80). Often stamps will advertise the natural resources of a country. Canada, for example, has issued many stamps showing its lumber, oil and mining industries, while coffee production has been a common theme for Latin American countries since the 1920s.

Developments in transport and communications seem particularly attractive to postal authorities, and most countries have stamps commemorating their national airlines and international airports. Not surprisingly, improvements in the postal service itself are an occasion for self-congratulation on stamps, expressed by honouring the postman or boasting of the introduction of postal codes and automatic sorting. Stamps encourage literacy, Western health methods and even, in the case of the central African country of Benin, the fight against witchcraft.

This emphasis on modernisation is also shown in the wide recognition of certain scientists and inventors on stamps — Alexander Graham Bell, Charles Darwin and Robert Koch (discoverer of the tuberculosis bacillus). Others are less favoured. Sigmund Freud has only appeared twice on a stamp: Austria, whence he had fled in 1938, marked his 125th anniversary in 1981, while Grenada included both Freud and Jung on a series for the 25th anniversary of the World Health Organisation in 1973. But then, psychoanalysis has very little to do with increasing gross national product, and is frowned upon by most authoritarian governments as potentially subversive.

SOUTH KOREA 1983

CHINA 1975

Since the launch of Sputnik in 1957, space exploration has become a staple of stamp design. Here is a subject that combines the glorification of technology, of national achievement and international co-operation with the opportunity for designers to make use of quite extraordinarily phallic imagery. In part this may explain the appeal of space exploration to boys, the major buyers of thematic stamp packets. It is little wonder that a whole collection of space stamps can be easily assembled. The Soviet Union, and to a lesser extent the United States, vaunt each achievement of their space programs on stamps — in a rare moment of co-operation the joint Soviet–American space project of 1975 was commemorated on stamps of both countries. Space exploration, too, is a way in which smaller countries can position themselves vis-à-vis the big powers, with many countries showing both Soviet and American expeditions (and Albania, but not China, honouring Chinese exploration). Neil Armstrong, "first man on the moon", in 1969, may be second only to Queen Elizabeth II among living people honoured on stamps. A checklist in 1975 showed he had been featured on the stamps of 56 countries, and there have been others since then.[15]

PARAGUAY 1970

ST LUCIA 1979

HUNGARY 1966

UNITED STATES OF AMERICA 1975

NICARAGUA 1981

**UNITED STATES OF AMERICA
1973; 1964**

Stamps as Propaganda for Good Citizenship

Stamps are inevitably conservative, in that they portray and foster official ideologies and pictures of the world. A certain number of stamps are deliberately exhoratory, invoking notions of good citizenship and appropriate behaviour. Thus, during World War II, Cuba issued stamps warning of the dangers of the Fifth Column. In the early 1950s, China encouraged home gymnastics with a series of stamps portraying the various exercises, and Venezuela has campaigned for tax payments by a series showing the benefits of government spending. A number of countries have issued stamps as part of literacy campaigns, some of which actually show letters of the alphabet in a manner reminiscent of *Sesame Street*.

The United States is particularly fond of appeals to good citizenship on its stamps and has used them to urge people to register to vote, to fight alcoholism, to give blood and, quite simply, invoking the word "love", an annual issue since 1982, since imitated by Ireland. Other countries do the same. There are increasing numbers of stamps aimed at alcoholism and drug abuse, at fighting pollution and road accidents, at saving energy and at encouraging breastfeeding. It is hard not to see a touch of hypocrisy — or, at least, optimism — in some of these stamps, such as those from the Bahamas, one of the main transit points for drug smuggling into the United States, boasting of "Customs co-operation". Or the Filipino stamp with the inscription "HELP ME STOP SMUGGLING, Pres. MARCOS".

Health concerns are frequent themes of stamps from the Third World, especially African countries, where stamps are used to urge immunisation, malaria control or the

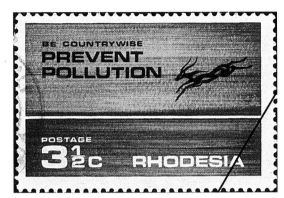

RHODESIA 1972

PHILIPPINES 1979

ISRAEL 1983

GHANA 1974

BAHAMAS 1983

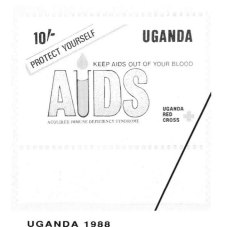

UGANDA 1988

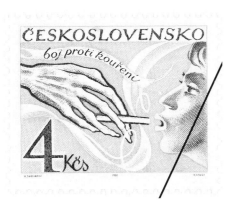

CZECHOSLOVAKIA 1981

SINGAPORE 1974

eradication of locusts. Uganda became the first country to encourage AIDS prevention campaigns on a stamp issued in 1988 — appropriately enough, as its case load per head is estimated as being among the highest in the world.

Susan Sontag has commented on the ways in which the campaign against tuberculosis after World War I drew heavily on military metaphors to arouse popular support for measures then believed effective.[16] These did not seem to directly affect stamp design, but certainly tuberculosis was a common theme for stamps, starting with a Dutch charity series of 1906. During the 1920s, 1930s and 1940s, numerous countries issued stamps for tuberculosis-related charities. And in other countries, without a tradition of charity stamps, tuberculosis societies issued Christmas seals to be used with Christmas mail. The only other illness to attract much philatelic attention in the inter-war years was cancer, for which there were also a number of charity and propaganda stamps, whereas the devastating influenza epidemic of 1919 seems to have escaped any philatelic recognition whatsoever.

After World War II, and especially after the growth of independent Third World countries, other diseases have featured on stamps, above all malaria. The 1962 global campaign against malaria was widely commemorated, as have been campaigns against smallpox and leprosy. More diffuse health concerns are reflected in the growing number of countries that have used stamps for anti-smoking propaganda, a far cry from the inter-war stamps of a number of tobacco-growing countries boasting of their production.

Family planning, although encouraged by many Third World governments, seems too controversial to make it on to many stamps, although China, India, Singapore and even South Africa have used the theme. The reverse message came from 1939 French charity stamps supporting the

MALI 1964

BELGIUM 1937

SOUTH AFRICA 1981;
GRENADA 1976

"Birth-rate development fund" at a time when war with Germany was looming, and Israel has issued a number of stamps celebrating Jewish immigration. And, yes, there are stamps for "motherhood", which emerges as a frequent theme on stamps in the 1930s and one that cuts across different ideological regimes. Motherhood was celebrated on a couple of stamps for Papua in 1932, was taken up in several Mother's Day issues by Austria between the wars and in a one-off United States issue in 1934. It is also referred to in a number of Nazi German stamps and is a theme on a number of charity stamps, such as this stamp from Belgium which makes use of the Royal family to endorse motherhood. The American stamp was apparently designed by President Roosevelt himself, his Postmaster General recalling that he drew it while sitting in bed and using Whistler's painting "Portrait of My Mother" as a model.[17] There have been a number of more recent stamps showing "motherhood" and celebrating Mother's Day (though none, as far as I know, for "fatherhood") and New Zealand issued a series of stamps in 1981 extolling "family life".

An important part of the theme of "good citizenship" are stamps supporting organisations of which governments approve, such as the Red Cross, Rotary and the Lions, Scouts and Guides, or their local variants. Official youth movements are particular favourites, since Hungary first issued a stamp showing Scouts in 1925, and they are popular with collectors. Liberia cashed in with a 50-stamp set based on Norman Rockwell's paintings of Scouts. Such topics can be seen both as examples of the internationalisation of Western values and organisations, and also of the creation of an official culture in which certain sorts of organisations are given priority. Thus, it is far more common to find stamps in Western countries extolling organisations such as Rotary or

SINGAPORE 1986

TUNISIA 1981

Chambers of Commerce than any form of social movement. During the 16 years that Sir Robert Menzies was Prime Minister, Australia issued nine stamps to commemorate volunteer organisations, including the Inland Mission and Country Women's Association, but none showing trade unions.

The line between promoting good citizenship and supporting a particular government is a fine one. Singapore has used stamps to promote approved community associations, the most recently featured of which are closely tied in to the ruling People's Action Party, as is the officially recognised trade union organisation (page 87). Similarly, the Malaysian stamps for International Women's Year showed the emblem of the Malayan Women's Organisation, which is closely linked to the ruling Malay party. Those countries with single political parties will often show them on stamps. In pluralist democracies the absence of political parties from stamps is almost total, although as long ago as 1896 Ecuador issued a series of stamps in honour of the Liberal Party, then the dominant — though not the only — party. A stamp proclaiming an electoral victory or the congress of a particular party (common in Communist countries, but the stamp on page 87 commemorates President Borguiba's Destoruian Socialist Party) is often a sign of political restrictions.

In different ways, stamps tend to show the ceremonial and the respectable, rather than the real face of power. Dictators are honoured, but not their secret police, constitutions and the rights of man, less often of women, proclaimed, but not concentration camps. While Western democracies tend to be more reticent about overt political themes, their choice of organisations and individuals to honour is itself political and almost always conservative: social and political movements are commemorated less often than military events. Thus, while Britain has acknowledged the Trades Union Congress and "social reformers" like Elizabeth Fry and Robert

Owen on its stamps, these are less common than the various stamps showing military and royal events.

Special note should be taken of the way in which the British Royals have become staples of stamp design in the post-War period. I have already mentioned the British practice of identifying their stamps by the image of the sovereign. (Ethiopia used the head of the Emperor Haile Selassie to a lesser extent in the 1950s and 1960s, and the African state of Gambia has adopted a similar practice since becoming a republic, depicting its president on every stamp.) For the first 100 years of stamps, the sovereign appeared on the stamps of Britain and its colonies as a symbol of the Empire and British rule, and, until 1964 and the Shakespeare Festival, no other identifiable person appeared on British stamps. It was dominions such as South Africa and Newfoundland that took the lead in showing other members of the Royal family, and the 1969 inauguration of Prince Charles as Prince of Wales was the first appearance on a British stamp of a Royal other than the King or Queen. Yet as more countries became independent and the Empire was replaced by the Commonwealth, there has been an increase, not a decrease, in royal themes on stamps. Between its independence in 1970 and the coup that took it out of the Commonwealth in 1987, Fiji issued stamps on at least nine occasions, to commemorate royal events.

MAURITIUS 1982;
COOK ISLANDS 1985

The coronations of both George VI and Elizabeth II, and the Silver Wedding of George and Elizabeth in 1949, produced commemorative issues throughout the Empire. They were modest compared to the orgy of commemoratives unleashed by the wedding of Prince Charles and Lady Diana in 1981 — and not only from the Commonwealth. The wedding was also an excuse for stamps from Bhutan, Ivory Coast, Niger, Paraguay and, as already mentioned,

**GREAT BRITAIN 1986;
LIBERIA 1981;
NORFOLK ISLAND 1986**

North Korea. Many of these countries followed with stamps for the birth of Prince William and the 21st birthday of the Princess three years later, hardly a major event, one would think, for the people of Liberia. More recently, there have been omnibus birthday issues for the Queen and the Queen Mother, whereby considerable numbers of British dependencies and Commonwealth members together produced miniature portrait histories of the Queens' lives; they also produced a large series for the wedding of Prince Andrew. However, there are limits to the philatelic marketing of the Royals. Buckingham Palace vetoed a move in 1985, by the British Virgin Islands, to put the Queen's head on a stamp showing pop star Michael Jackson.

Like St Vincent, the Virgin Islands went ahead with the stamp anyway, perhaps with the calculation that Jackson would be a bigger drawcard in the shops than the Queen. As pop stars and movie actors have appeared on stamps in increasing numbers, it is only a period of time before whole episodes of Dynasty *follow.*

ST VINCENT 1984

God and the Post

Not surprisingly, religion is a common theme for stamps, particularly where there are established or state religions. Religious themes were already common in the 19th century. The first issue of the British Virgin Islands in the West Indies in 1866 showed portraits of St Ursula and of the Madonna and Child — very appropriate given the name of the islands (the original name of the colony was "St Ursula and Her Companions"). Malta commemorated St Paul's shipwreck on the island on one of its earlier stamps, in 1899, and like Belgium, Ireland, the Philippines and some Latin American countries, has produced large numbers of stamps showing Catholic saints and events.

Franco's Spain stands out for its frequent use of Catholic images, and, particularly, the calculated linking of such religious symbols with those of the state. Few stamps show this as clearly as this issue, one of a series for the 50th anniversary of Spanish aviation. The stamp shows the patron saint, the Madonna of Loreto.

SPAIN 1961

Islamic references are frequent on stamps from Saudi Arabia and Pakistan, and Buddhist themes are common on Sri Lankan stamps. What is more interesting is the way in which more secular societies deal with religion, and the careful balancing of different religious sects that is sometimes required.

To avoid controversy, many countries either downplay specific religious themes, or else adopt pluralism as the basis for stamp design. In 1968 Guyana issued stamps for Christmas, for the anniversary of the Koran and for the Hindu

Festival of Phagwah. One of Zanzibar's independence issues, in 1963, was specifically on the theme of "religious tolerance". A number of countries with Catholic majorities have honoured Freemasonry with stamps, for example, Belgium, Brazil and Honduras, despite Catholic opposition to the organisation. (The German puppet state of Serbia issued specifically anti-masonic stamps during World War II, one of the few examples of sectarian propaganda on stamps.) Largely Muslim Jordan has issued stamps depicting the Stations of the Cross. The United States has mostly avoided religious themes in deference to the Constitutional separation of church and state, although a stamp was issued in 1983 to commemorate the 500th anniversary of Martin Luther's birth, reputedly after President Reagan's adviser (later Attorney General) Edwin Meese, relayed a message from his pastor to the President.

Most Western countries maintain a certain degree of separation between church and state. The United States, while issuing Christmas stamps each year since 1963, always includes one non-religious design and Australia explicitly prohibits "anniversaries or events connected with religious organisations". But Britain, while never having acknowledged the established Anglican Church, has issued a stamp to commemorate the centenary of the Salvation Army, Sweden has produced a set of stamps honouring various Protestant denominations, Belgium has honoured both its Protestant minority and the Papal Encyclical "Rerum Novarum", and West Germany has produced a number of stamps with religious themes, carefully balanced between Protestant and Catholic leanings.

Christmas stamps have become widespread, with even countries such as Communist-ruled Cuba and Hungary, and largely Buddhist Sri Lanka, issuing them. (A variant on the Christmas stamp is the annual issue of a New Year's stamp

JORDAN 1966

GHANA 1977

in Japan, which is used to ensure that cards bearing that stamp are delivered on 1 January.) One sees in the proliferation of these stamps the diffusion of Western imagery, as in the religious art used on a number of African stamps. There are also examples of local traditions being drawn on for Christmas designs, in images of local dance and festivals. Of stamps celebrating the achievements of Western missionaries, nowhere has this been as pronounced as in the largely Muslim Dutch East Indies (now Indonesia) where during the 1930s large numbers of stamps were issued for various Protestant causes such as the Salvation Army, the YMCA and the Christian Military Home.

The Vatican is, of course, a special case in the issuing of religious stamps. As the Papal States, between 1852 and 1870 when it was conquered by the Italian army, it issued stamps, all displaying the papal insignia. Following the Lateran Treaty of 1929, which established the Vatican as a separate state within the city of Rome, it has had its own postal service — often used by Romans because of its alleged greater reliability than the Italian — and its stamps reflect totally the

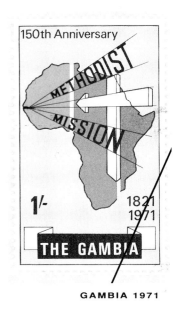

GAMBIA 1971

VATICAN CITY 1984

doctrines and concerns of the Catholic Church. The constant travelling of Pope John Paul II has produced increasing numbers of stamps commemorating his trips (see previous page). Other than the occasional recognition of some non-religious celebrity — Copernicus and Gregor Mendel have both appeared on Vatican stamps — its stamps reflect the official face of Catholicism. To some extent, post-Pahlavi Iran and Israel can be classed alongside the Vatican because of their strong emphasis on religious themes.

Lobbying: Fighting for Stamps of One's Own

The Luther stamp issued by the US illustrates the politics that lie behind the issuing of a number of stamps. The United States, like a number of countries, has stamp advisory committees. In the Luther case, as in others, their role seems to have been sidestepped. In the United States, up to 1500 suggestions a year are made for the 20 to 30 subjects that will get a stamp of their own, and there are not infrequent examples of interference by politicians. Roosevelt and Truman both influenced certain choices of stamp topics, and under Truman there was a flood of stamps for special interests, including the poultry industry, the American Bankers' Association, the American Automobile Association and even a private company, the Baltimore and Ohio Railway. One can see the interests of a Presidential wife, Lady Bird Johnson, reflected in these 1969 stamps for the "beautification of America".

More recently, the current set of "great Americans" has been particularly open to lobbying by ethnic communities. When the Postal Service announced a stamp honouring Bernard Revel, first head of Yeshiva University in New York,

PLANT for more BEAUTIFUL CITIES

PLANT for more BEAUTIFUL PARKS

PLANT for more BEAUTIFUL HIGHWAYS

PLANT for more BEAUTIFUL STREETS

30627

UNITED STATES OF AMERICA 1969

it was an occasion for special celebration by the University.[18]
Since 1970 there has been a series of stamps honouring American poets, the idea for which came from Marie Bullock,
founder of the Academy of American poets, and the Carter
administration initiated a series of stamps showing prominent black Americans and commemorating "Black heritage",
which the Reagan administration continued. Any pressure
group, it would seem, if sufficiently well-organised and determined, can get "its" stamp in the United States. One will
sometimes see letters in American newspapers exhorting people to write to the Stamp Advisory Committee in support of
recognition for some person or event. Supports and detractors
of a stamp in honour of Elvis Presley — already on the stamps
of six countries, including St Vincent, Malagasy and West
Germany — are particularly vociferous.

Lobbying for stamp subjects is not, of course,
confined to the United States. Australian Liberal Senator
Chris Puplick, himself a stamp collector, has detailed how
Parliamentary pressure forced Australia Post to issue a stamp

ST VINCENT 1987

PAPUA NEW GUINEA 1970

commemorating the meeting of the Commonwealth Parliamentary Association in Canberra in 1988.[19] Even corporations
have occasionally achieved recognition through stamps, as in
the Filipino stamps for anniversaries of the Hong Kong and
Shanghai Banking Corporation and of several foreign airlines. Who sits on advisory committees will, of course, influence content. It has been suggested to me that Papua New
Guinea's stamps prior to independence in 1975 were strongly
influenced by anthropologists — hence all those stamps of
native artefacts and dwellings, with even a stamp showing the
doyen of Pacific anthropologists, Malinowski.

Propaganda —
National Celebration

Virtually all stamps either reflect a pseudo-internationalism (one aimed essentially at stamp collectors in the rich First World), or represent the celebration of the nation state and its symbols. The growing tendency of countries in search of hard currency to produce stamps for the external market makes analysis difficult. One can say little about the corrupt politics of Zaire based on an analysis of stamps showing locomotives, football and Norman Rockwell paintings. But even where overseas marketing requirements are dominant, other factors are involved. North Korea, for example, has mixed its veneration of Kim Il Sung with stamps aimed firmly at the young collectors of the imperialist world.

In other cases stamps most often convey the most anodyne components of what Horne termed "the public culture", claiming a contrived consensus around such "non-political" symbols as animals and flowers. Even here, however, one can quite often find a political significance. Stamps showing animals, one of the most common of all designs, may be also showing national symbols, as in the early use of beavers on Canadian stamps, or the polar bear on those of Greenland, or emblems of commercial production (sheep, cattle etc.), or paradigms of domestic values (pet cats and dogs), or parts of national tourist attractions (as in the big game depicted on many African stamps), or support for conservation campaigns, or themes in local art. Most of the early stamps of the Sudan depicted a postman riding a camel, a design that combines references to the traditional use of animals for communications, with a particular image of national identity, just as China uses its pandas or Western

Australia used its black swan. After its Bicentennial orgy in 1988, Australia turned to themes with no apparent political content for its 1989 issues — sport, sheep, gardens, trams and "footlights and the flickering films". Yet these issues are clearly part of the construction of a certain sort of Australian nationalism. Unlike Zaire, say, or Grenada, the paintings and the trams on Australian stamps are not from outside the country, and Australia Post is more influenced by the tastes of domestic philatelists than of foreign.

One of the earliest extra-postal uses of stamps was to promote an interest in the tourist attractions of the issuing country. Already in the 19th century scenic views appeared on the stamps of a number of countries, ranging from Montenegro to Tasmania and the Belgian Congo. In the period between the two World Wars, one can see a quite conscious link to tourist promotion in French stamps, showing such attractions as the famous abbey, the Mont St Michel, off the coast of Brittany and the "ski-ing week" at Mont Blanc in the Alps. Holidays for working-class families were one of the major demands of the left in this period, symbolised in charity stamps aimed at supporting the "postal workers' sports fund".

Many other countries have linked their stamp issues to tourist promotion, as in regular issues from Japan, which since the 1930s has shown its National Parks on stamps, New Zealand and a number of tropical island states. After all, the majority of stamps used on overseas mail from places like the Maldives or the Cayman Islands will be on postcards from Western tourists, and hence might as well be used for promotional purposes. Some stamps have become, in effect, tourist posters in miniature (see page 100). A series of Portuguese stamps in 1971 showing old windmills, conveniently located the mills in trilingual inscriptions on the back of each

JAPAN 1938

DRAVUNI BEACH

Fiji Tourism 45c

FIJI 1970

stamp. One consequence of this promotion of tourism is the quite frequent appearance of international hotels on stamps, including those of most major chains. The Indian Ocean island of the Seychelles, in 1981, showed all its large international hotels on a series of stamps proclaiming, "Seychelles: Unique by a Thousand Miles".

Large numbers of stamps now depict recreational activities aimed at encouraging visitors, often (as with the 1987 New Zealand set, right) issued in the denominations needed for overseas postage. Of course, only the respectable face of tourism is shown. Gambling is only occasionally acknowledged (Monaco, at least, has shown its casino on a stamp), and prostitution never. Americans may flock to Nassau for the casinos, but the Bahamas is more inclined to depict churches on its stamps.

With some exceptions, to be discussed as issues of design rather than content, stamps are very conservative products that venerate the most respectable version of social reality. Depending on the dominant ideology, the conservatism may be expressed through appeals to nostalgia, as in the case of

Australian sheep or British army uniforms, or in the language of progress — all those Third World and Communist stamps proclaiming peace and more tractors. But in both cases the public culture is reaffirmed. There are nice examples of both sorts of conservatism in stamps from African countries, which increasingly commemorate traditional culture alongside new buildings and airports. Common to all these themes, along with many scenic views and native animals, is the consolidation of national consensus around agreed-upon symbols which, in almost all cases, deny uncomfortable differences of class, race or belief.

Increasingly, this consensus means a homogeneity in the subject of stamps. Since the 1950s, when the countries of Eastern Europe led by Hungary, began producing large number of stamps aimed at the collectors of hard currency states, a Eurocentric universalism has permeated more and more of the world's stamps, bearing out Marshall McLuhan's contention that in the "global village" there is simultaneously a strengthening of the specific and the universal. To make a sweeping generalisation, this is probably least apparent in the larger countries of the Middle East and North Africa, where propaganda is more crucial a criterion than philatelic revenue. As foreshadowed earlier, there has been a marked increase in what is seen as "fit and proper" subject matter for stamps, but however broad the new definition — with stamps showing movie actors and pirate adventures — stamps remain clearly part of the public culture, acting to celebrate power and control subversion.

NEW ZEALAND 1986

1. R. Williams, *Towards 2000*, Chatto & Windus, London, 1982, p. 192.
2. For more details see P. Beck, "Argentina's 'Philatelic Annexation' of the Falklands", *History Today*, February 1983, pp. 39–44.
3. B. Hornadge, *Stamps: A Collector's Guide*, Sun Books, Melbourne, 1968, p. 12.
4. E. Pollock (ed), "Famous Stamps and Their Stories", *Globus Stamps*, New York, 1938.
5. Memo from A. Currall, Managing Director Post Office, to David Le B. Jones, Department of Industry, 19 February 1975.

6. S. Phillips, *Stamp Collecting*, Sampson Low, London, 1932, pp. 36-7.

7. Commonwealth Parliamentary Debates, 21 August 1913.

8. See D.C. Skaggs, "Postage Stamps as Icons" in R. Browne and M. Fishwick, *Icons of America*, Popular Press, Bowling Green, Ohio, 1978.

9. See Patrick Wright, *On Living in an Old Country*, Verso, London, 1985.

10. See the discussion in H. McQueen, "The Australian Stamp", *Arena*, no. 84, 1988.

11. Charles Stewart, Etymologies of Power", review of M. Herzfeld's *Anthropology Through the Looking-Glass*, *Times Literary Supplement*, 6–12 January 1989, p. 18.

12. J. Dunn, "Stamps", *New York Times*, 23 June 1985.

13. I. Buruma, "Playing for Keeps", *New York Review of Books*, 10 November 1988.

14. D. Horne, *The Public Culture*, Pluto, London, 1986, p.77.

15. C.E. Wagner (ed), *Americana on Foreign Stamps*, American Topical Association, Milwaukee, 1975. This is an oddly chauvinistic catalogue, as it lists many stamps showing an international event or organisation as part of "Americana".

16. S. Sontag, *AIDS and Its Metaphors*, Farrar, Strauss & Giroux, New York, 1988, p.10.

17. J. Farley, *Behind the Ballots*, Harcourt, Brace, New York, 1938, p. 338.

18. "New Stamp Will Honor First Head of Yeshiva U", *New York Times*, 10 September 1985.

19. C. Puplick, "Stamping on Australia Post", *The House Magazine*, Canberra, 13 April 1988.

ISSUES OF STYLE AND AESTHETICS

Stamps must carry a clear message in an artistic way that will be easily understood. They should appeal to everyone because they can be one of the best propaganda materials of all. George Hamori quoted in *Treasury of Stamps*

Stamps have rarely been considered as art forms, although under British Postmaster General Tony Benn's influence, the Royal College of Art appointed a Fellow in Stamp Design in 1966. In general, the aesthetic value of stamps has always been subordinated to the political and financial requirements of governments, and where stamps succeed as works of art, it tends to be in spite of, rather than because of, conscious policy.

The early stamps tended to be small, rectangular and of one colour. But there have been as many variations on the basic design parameters as human ingenuity can devise. The first stamps of the Cape of Good Hope (1853) were triangular in shape, in order to assist postal clerks in sorting inland from overseas letters. The first from British Guiana (1850) and Afghanistan (1893) were circular, a shape recently revived by both New Zealand and Malaysia. The Pacific island

TONGA 1978

of Tonga produces self-adhesive stamps, impossible to soak off envelopes, in a variety of shapes and sizes, as has Sierra Leone. Stamps have been issued on the backs of old banknotes and maps (Latvia, due to post-World War I paper shortages), on artificial silk (Poland) and on tinfoil (Paraguay).

Stamps have become, on the whole, larger than in the 19th century, with Guatemala issuing a stamp in 1984 that is almost half the size of the average paperback. Two-colour stamps were already being produced last century, but multi-coloured issues have become standard in past decades, as have increasing numbers of issues where different stamps are joined in pairs or strips, sometimes telling a story or making up a composite picture. A variant of this is the miniature sheet, where the stamp itself is set within a much larger piece of paper conveying a design. The United States now issues considerable numbers of stamps in blocks or strips of four or five, with different designs around a common theme. In 1976, it produced a sheet of 50 stamps, showing all the state flags, a device since used for both birds and animals — and one responsible for greatly increasing the annual number of US issues. By the end of the 1980s, the Himalayan state of Bhutan was issuing 3-D stamps, which are non-adhesive and have no apparent postal purpose.

A great deal of effort is expended on stamp design, even if the end result often does not reflect this. Nevertheless, contemporary stamps from countries such as Japan, West Germany, Greece and the Netherlands reflect very high standards of graphic art, as did some of the French colonial issues earlier. In general, however, the design of stamps is conservative, and tends to lag behind current developments in design, as would be expected on official products. This seems most apparent in the case of American stamps, generally regarded as including some of the worst designs of all major countries.

The postal and political requirements of stamps, and their very smallness, places constraints on designers that remain even in the age of large, odd-shaped and garish issues. As the Irish designer Louis le Brocquy remarked, "I have always found it surprising that the first and second stamps ever issued, Britain's Penny Black and Two Pence Blue, 1840, hit the right normal shape and size to which all stamps have subsequently tended to revert."[1] And as another designer, the Tunisian Hatim Elmekki, added, "Sometimes I suffer the constraints of conventional subjects: how can one, for example, design an elevating stamp showing the president inaugurating an exposition of chrysanthemums?"[2]

I have found it impossible to locate any extended analysis of the aesthetics and design of postage stamps as exists, for example, for posters (themselves the subject of some stamps). To the best of my knowledge, none of our contemporary decoders of cultural signs — neither Roland Barthes nor Susan Sontag, for example — have written about the manifold signs contained within stamps. Philatelists seem remarkably uninterested in informed discussion of design, and few students of the fine arts have thought to include stamps in their purview. The closest I have found in English is a section in an American illustrated book on stamps and a chapter in James Watson's book on stamps and stamp collecting.[3] The subject has been dealt with more seriously in German[4] and possibly other languages as well.

The most common writings on the subject are throwaway comments in the columns of philatelic magazines, usually complaining about anything that is innovative, and there is the odd tribute to individual artists, such as a chapter in a book on the New Zealander James Berry, who dominated stamp design in his native country for 40 years, and who also designed stamps for Bermuda, Tonga, the Cook Islands and

BELGIUM 1973

Western Samoa.[5] There are also a few pages in David Gentleman's *Design in Miniature*[6] that deal entirely with British stamps and his experience as a designer in the 1960s. The comments that follow are written in the hope of encouraging a more systematic and informed analysis of the aesthetics of stamp design, and the appreciation of stamps as works of art.

The first stamps, as we have seen, showed either the head of the sovereign or some symbol of national unity, and often drew on what was considered appropriate for coins. The head of Queen Victoria on the Penny Black was copied from a medal struck to mark her first official visit to the City of London after her coronation in 1838. It has been suggested that one reason for using the sovereign's head was that it made forgery more difficult than would, say, a purely abstract design.[7]

The design of the earliest stamps, and of most of those that followed, can be seen as either emblematic or neo-realist. The first type are designs that use symbols, often of the nation state, and include a whole range of heroic designs much favoured at the turn of the century, but by no means discarded: designs using beacons and torches are continuing favourites. France has made frequent use of allegorical images representing "the spirit of war", "the provinces" and "France" herself, but such devices have been used by almost all countries at some point.

The neo-realist stamp encompasses natural views, pictures of animals and plants, portraits or historical scenes — all those stamps where the emphasis is on a fairly accurate depiction of the subject. Thus the inset of the Queen's head on the side of all British stamps is emblematic, but the reproductions of photographs of her and of the Queen Mother in the multi-state series commemorating their birthdays, are neo-realist. Paintings and photographs are obviously the basis for

**TURKEY 1960;
ITALY 1945**

large numbers of stamp designs and increasingly there is an emphasis on accurate representation on stamps. Photogravure methods of stamp production were first used in Bavaria in 1913, but did not become common until after World War II. Usually the direct reproduction of photographs is less effective than paintings based upon photos.

Early stamp issues drew heavily on paintings for their designs. The first US issues included portraits of George Washington drawn from paintings by Americans Gilbert Stuart and John Turnbull, and from a bust by the French sculptor, Jean Antoine Houdon, the contemporary equivalent to a court photographer. Using stamps to show "great paintings" was an obvious development already adopted on some stamps of the 1920s. Art depicted on stamps tends to fall clearly into the realm of "the public culture", although some countries such as France, Austria and the Netherlands, have been reasonably adventurous in depicting contemporary art. Others, such as Australia, claim to experience buyer resistance to anything but the most traditional of designs. Both China and Japan have, in recent years, used stamps to display some of their traditional art to considerable effect, and a number of countries, such as India, Cuba and the Soviet Union, have used children's drawings on their stamps.

The choice of paintings for reproduction on stamps has not been without its controversies. Most famous is probably the Spanish issue in 1930 marking the art of Goya (page 108). Tirades of abuse were aimed at the Spanish authorities, most of it in the name of "the innocent children" who collected stamps. Much less attention had been paid to the stamps showing bare-breasted women on some African and Pacific stamps, showing the double

**JAPAN 1980;
CHINA 1987**

SPAIN 1930

CYPRUS 1979

standards of racism in such matters. There was a faint echo of this controversy in 1940 when the United States reproduced Botticelli's "Three Graces" on a stamp honouring the Pan American Union, and the diaphanous clothing of the three women — representing North, Central and South America — led to rumours that the stamp would be withdrawn from circulation. Today nudes are just another design aimed at collectors, as in these stamps from Cyprus. Nudes are generally female, a reflection of male dominance in art, but there are also a number of homoerotic designs in stamps, particularly those depicting near-naked wrestlers. Acute readers might notice several homoerotic references in earlier illustrations, but because these must always remain covert, with no state being prepared to acknowledge the possibility on their stamps, there is great scope for interpretation. I have seen several works of art incorporating stamps showing male athletes, which thereby heighten their sexuality.[8]

FRANCE 1925

AUSTRIA 1922

Stamp designers have been influenced by different artistic fashions and national traditions. The first stamps of the Turkish Empire and of the Hejaz (now Saudi Arabia) were elaborate ornamental designs showing the influence of Islamic design. Art Deco, art nouveau and constructivism can all be found as influences upon stamp design. One of the major exponents of art nouveau, the Czech painter, Alfons Mucha, designed his country's first stamps in 1918, showing a view of the Prague Castle in appropriately ornate framing (page 110). The 1920s was a period of considerable artistic experimentation, which is reflected in a proliferation of stamp styles during the period, with interesting examples coming particularly from European countries such as Belgium and the Netherlands, and from South America.

Many collectors would argue that the stamps of the inter-war years have a detail and dignity that is rarely matched today. The elaborate borders and allegorical designs once popular, especially for airmail stamps, have been replaced by

MEXICO 1939

CZECHOSLOVAKIA 1918

**MADAGASCAR 1930;
UNITED STATES OF AMERICA
1939**

**WEST GERMANY 1986;
CYPRUS 1977**

stamps that are simpler and more representational, although one also finds more adventurous designs that verge on the abstract or even minimalist. Some modern stamps deliberately use one colour as a reaction against the garishness of so many issues, or employ black and white imagery, as in this powerful appeal for refugees from Cyprus (below left).

There are, of course, other forms that may be used for stamp design. Cartoons and caricatures are increasingly found on stamps with Australia, France and the Netherlands most attracted to this style. In 1988 Australia Post released a major set of definitives drawn by a collection of the country's best known cartoonists, with the theme "Living Together". There was considerable controversy surrounding some of the submitted designs, which showed children playing doctors (for health), and roadworkers behind the sign "Persons at Work" (for unions) — both were rejected[9] — and the series proved unpopular with collectors, who tend to be very literal in their tastes. Caricatures sometimes take the place of more orthodox portraits, as in the Irish issue that matched the shape of the stamps to the shape of Bernard Shaw and Oscar Wilde, its two greatest ironists, respectively. Recently, several

ITALY 1983

BOLIVIA 1986

NETHERLANDS 1978

AUSTRALIA 1975

AUSTRALIA 1988

IRELAND 1980

UNITED STATES
OF AMERICA 1986

ST JOHN AMBULANCE 1887-1987
TRANSPLANT ORGAN FLIGHT 1987

GREAT BRITAIN 1987

countries, led by the United States, have adopted a greeting card style for some stamps, largely for marketing purposes.

Style can often echo politics, as in the nostalgic designs of some British stamps under Thatcher where there is a deliberate reversion to older design styles to emphasise a particular view of the past, or as in the photo-realism of many contemporary stamps. In some cases, such as Maoist China or Nazi Germany, regimes bring certain official theories about art to bear on stamp design. Stamps issued by Nazi Germany reflected certain precepts of the regime, with images of "pure" German youths and Aryan mothers on stamps (page 114). The return of the Saar following the plebescite of 1935 was depicted as a child returning to his (blonde) mother, and there was some invocation of classical mythology, sometimes in the form of heroic statues of horses, which has been identified as a popular form for Nazi art.[10] The Fascist accession to power in Italy meant not only stamps whose themes referred back to classical Rome, but a sort of ersatz Roman look to many other of its stamps, even for topics such as an inter-university sports contest (page 114). In the stamps Italy issued for its African colonies, Eritrea, Libya, Somalia and Ethiopia (after 1936),

INDIA 1985;
EAST GERMANY 1988

GERMANY 1944

ITALIAN EAST AFRICA 1938

LIBYA 1938

ITALY 1933

one sees fascist pomposity at its height, replete with references to Imperial Rome and grandiose architecture.

Stamps are, unfortunately, all too often characterised by the sort of art that Robert Hughes called "the narcissism of power", namely art that acts so as to glorify official regimes and (male) authority. One associates such stamps with the mock heroism of fascist Italy and the socialist realism of Stalinist Russia, only gradually being modified by *glasnost*. They are, however, far more widespread; "the narcissism of power" shows itself not only in the statues and monuments that glorify particular nationalisms and regimes, such as Zimbabwe's commemoration of Heroes' Day — the memorial that is featured was designed by a team of North Korean artists and sculptors — but also in the stylised athletes and phallic structures of many issues.

Gradually, there is some recognition that stamp design is, in fact, a form of art, and there are several

IN COMMEMORATION OF HEROES' DAYS — 11th and 12th AUGUST 1984

ZIMBABWE 1984

TURKEY 1960;
BULGARIA 1971

international competitions for the best design, mainly run by European organisations, such as the Viennese-based WIPA. Some countries depend on a stable of artists. The South Korean, Kangh Choon Whan, has been responsible for most of his country's stamps since 1959 and many of Japan's most striking stamps are designed by S. Watanabe.[11]

Other countries have commissioned stamps from artists famous in other media, as when the British Post Office asked the cartoonist Ralph Steadman to design stamps for the appearance of Halley's Comet, or Mexico's use of some of the works of Diego Rivera. In many cases, states will seek stamp designs through competition, a practice often used by the United Nations.

As printing requirements for multi-coloured stamps are quite complex, there are certain centres where a large range of stamps are produced; London (particularly Harrison and Sons and the House of Questa), Switzerland (especially the firm of Courvoisier), Paris, and Vienna are traditional centres for stamp production. Sometimes politics will dictate where stamps are printed. Some Third World countries are now using the services of the Hungarian State Printing Office, while for a long period Israel's influence in some African countries was reflected in its production of most of Togo's stamps.[12] Some countries have very distinctive "looks" to their stamps, such as Czechoslovakia and Sweden, which are among the few countries to use recess printing as against the more common line-engraving and photogravure processes. Swedish stamps have been described as "having a striking terseness and stylisation"[13] and, like the stamps of other Scandinavian countries, are noticeably more subdued than the garish issues of many countries (see right). Sweden runs an annual mail competition to seek public reactions to its stamp designs.

Oddly enough, it is the few artists who have turned to the creation of imaginary stamps who have done most to make people aware of the artistic possibilities of stamp design. The American artist, Donald Evans, spent much of his short life (1945–77) designing a growing collection of imaginary stamps for imaginary countries.[14] These included countries such as a coral archipelago, *Amis et Amants* (friends and lovers); the Arctic country of *Yteke*, named after a Dutch dancer, and the *Iles des Sourds* (Isles of the Deaf) (page 118). His designs were described by the British travel writer, Bruce Chatwin, as making up "a limpid, luminous world — a kind of Baudelairean *pays de Cocagne* (land of plenty) — that would mirror his own life and the life of his times."[15] Other artists have used the form of imaginary stamps to make political comments. The French artist Carelman published a "Catalogue of Unfindable Stamps", which included an apartheid issue for South Africa, the same design in black and white versions, but with the black one, one-tenth the size of the white; stamps proclaiming the joy of hashish from Nepal and a common French design as it might have been drawn by Picasso, Leger and Matisse.[16] A similar set of false stamps from the United States commemorated such "blessings of American life" as "cheese-flavoured dog food" and "heated shaving cream".[17] Some contemporary artists, for example Andy Warhol, have used stamps within art works to explore concepts of ubiquity and the division between "high" and "pop" art.[18]

More and more countries, in their search for the collectors' dollar, turn to foreign agencies for their stamps. Thus Disney cartoons are issued by a score of post offices, and scenic views are drawn by artists who have only photographs to guide them. Nonetheless, the standard of design of at least some stamps merits more attention from art critics than it has yet received.

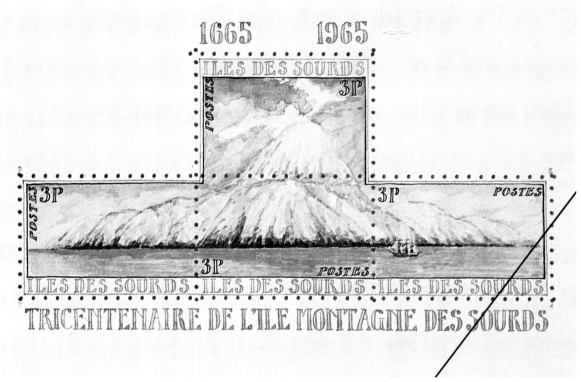

DONALD EVANS:
"TERCENTENARY OF THE ISLAND MOUNTAIN OF THE DEAF"
POSTCARD, STEDEIJK MUSEUM, AMSTERDAM

1. D. Lidman, *Treasury of Stamps*, Harry Abrams, New York, 1975, p. 122.
2. *ibid*, p. 299.
3. Lidman *op cit*; J. Watson, *The Stanley Gibbons Book of Stamps and Stamp Collecting*, Windward, London, 1981.
4. Richard Peck has drawn my attention to the *Archiv für Deutsche Postgeshichte*, published in Frankfurt, and articles such as H.R. Johannsen ad O. Brauns-Packenius, "Die Briefmarke — ein grapfisches Kunstwerk", *Archiv* 2/77. Similar works exist in Dutch.
5. J.W. Brodie, "James Berry — Stamp Designer" in J.R. Tye (ed), *The Image Maker*, Hodder and Stoughton, Auckland, 1984.
6. D. Gentleman, *Design in Miniature*, Studio Vista, London, 1972.
7. See J. Mackay, *Commonwealth Stamp Design 1840–1965*, British Museum, London, 1965, p. 9.
8. See S. Holt and C. McAuliffe (eds), *Imaging AIDS*, Melbourne, 1988 published in conjunction with the Australian Centre for Contemporary Art, for a reproduction of a Portuguese Timor stamp within an artwork by Malcolm Enright (1988) entitled "Another Inseparable: Person/Compassion".
9. L. Nicklin, "Elusive Stamp of Approval", the *Bulletin*, 22 March 1988, pp. 52–55.
10. B. Hinz, *Art in the Third Reich*, Blackwell, Oxford, 1974, p. 161.
11. L. Mucha and B. Hlinka, *The Orbis Philatelic Atlas*, Orbis, London, 1987.
12. J. Alden, *Printers and Printing in Philately*, Picton Publishing, Chippenham, 1976, p. 56.
13. *ibid*, p. 158. For more on the details of stamp production see Alden *ibid*; Watson *op cit*; and P. Thorp, *A Guide to Stamp Collecting*, Minkus, New York, 1972, pp. 57–71.
14. See W. Eisenhart, *The World of Donald Evans*, Harlin Quist, New York, 1981.
15. B. Chatwin, "The Album of Donald Evans", *New York Review of Books*, 14 May 1981, pp. 14–16.
16. Carelman, *Catalogue de Timbres-poste Introuvable*, Ballard, Paris, 1972.
17. B. McCall, *Bruce Mc'Call's Zany Afternoons*, Picador, London, 1983.
18. For an example of this from a feminist perspective see Julie Brown-Rrap, "Fred McCubbin on the Wallaby Track 1986/Julie Brown-Rrap on the Bandwagon 1988", installation photographs, reproduced in P. Foss (ed), *Island in the Stream*, Pluto, Sydney, 1988, pp. 108–9.

SWEDEN 1976; 1972; 1983

CHAPTER FIVE
COLLECTORS AND MONEY

Collecting ... is an activity that is not quite normal, there are no logical reasons why you do it. They can come later. Bruce Chatwin *Utz*

I have collected stamps since I was a small boy, with varying degrees of interest, even obsession. From my father I learnt to prize used stamps above unused, to be suspicious of stamps that seemed too pretty, and to arrange countries by geographic locations rather than names, because names of countries change too fast.

Most boys, far fewer girls, collect stamps at some point but most of them give up in their teens. As the Australian author Angelo Loukakis wrote, "A traitor to my origins, I suppose, I was much keener on British Empire stamps than I was on Greek or European ones ... But stamp collecting, like nicking off after school, ended for me a long time ago. And the Queen no longer matters except as a side-show, and the British Empire has vanished..."[1] However, the Empire is far from dead philatelically, as we've already seen, and many thousands of collectors persist with their hobby into adulthood — or, indeed, take it up later in life. But stamp collecting in the 1990s is a far different hobby from the one I adopted in the 1950s.

Almost all of the precepts by which I started to collect now seem out of date. Collecting, which was once a matter of begging for stamps from other people's mail — I remain fond of rummaging through wastepaper baskets for discarded stamps — has now become a business whereby collectors have standing orders from various postal authorities for their new issues, and stamps go straight from printing presses to the safe deposit boxes of collectors, often completely avoiding their nominal country of origin. Elements of my childhood experience remain, particularly in Europe, where open-air stamp markets still exist. But more and more, stamp collecting has been commercialised and the serendipity of an odd find — a postcard, say, from the Bahamas or some old envelope from an aunt's attic — is of little interest to the contemporary collector.

Maybe it is pure nostalgia that makes me hanker for the old-style grab-bag type of collecting. It is clearly impossible, without enormous resources, to collect the total number of stamps (nearly 10,000 by the 1990s) that appear each year. Specialisation makes sense. So too does the idea of collecting by theme, for instance railways, flowers, musicians, or Catholic saints. The most popular themes, according to various surveys of stamp collectors, are animals, space ships and flowers, but there are more exotic specialities — one shop lists 69 categories, including chess, minerals and stamps on stamps. Increasingly collectors seem to fall into one of two sorts: thematic or single country collectors, who buy most of their stamps via standing orders with philatelic agencies and who are only interested in mint issues; and philatelists, those who spend a lifetime in the increasingly arcane study of one or two particular periods or even issues.

Modern capitalism has incorporated stamp collecting in a way that is extremely frustrating for the determined amateur who wants to spend hours browsing through neighbourhood stamp shops in search of a missing 1937 issue. Real estate booms in our large cities have forced most dealers to work by mail rather than from shops. The last time I looked for stamp shops in downtown Sydney most had disappeared along with their buildings, and post offices have adopted modern marketing techniques to sell their products, with less and less pretence that stamps have anything to do with providing a postal service.

PITCAIRN ISLANDS 1940

The Philatelic Market

Increasingly the post offices of the world produce far more stamps than are needed for either postal or propaganda purposes, aiming them at stamp collectors, but this is not a new practice. Liberia and North Borneo were allegedly producing stamps partly for international collectors by the beginning of the century. Between the two World Wars, various small European states, such as Liechtenstein, San Marino and the Italian-occupied Aegean Islands (which included Rhodes) issued far more stamps than were needed, partly with an eye to collectors. The first stamps produced in 1940 for the Pitcairn Islands, a British possession in the Pacific, were issued less for postal use by the inhabitants (who then numbered under 200) than for those collectors who had become aware of the islands with the release of the film *Mutiny on the Bounty* based on the story of Captain Bligh. The descendants of the mutineers still

RWANDA 1971;
TURKS & CAICOS ISLANDS 1979;
FUJEIRA 1970

inhabit the island. One author claims the colonial postal authorities made more out of the mutiny with these stamps, than did either the film or the book.[2] (The Pacific island of Tonga, never slow to cash in on a philatelic gimmick, issued its own stamps showing scenes from the film in 1985.)

Since World War II more and more countries, including some quite wealthy ones, have greatly stepped up the production of stamps for philatelic sales. The most extreme cases were from the various states of the northern Arabian peninsula which, since 1972, have made up the United Arab Emirates. In the period between 1963 and 1972, these sheikhdoms issued thousands of stamps with no other use than sale to credulous collectors. The world record for stamp issue is held by Ajman, which managed to produce 448 stamps in one year alone. Almost all the stamps produced by places such as Fujeira, Khor Fakkan and Umm Al-Qiwain, ended up in stamp packets bought by children, as is true for the other stamps illustrated above. Since these sheikhdoms ended their separate existence, the most notorious offenders are certain Pacific and Caribbean islands, such as Tuvalu (formerly the Ellice Islands) and the Grenadines of St Vincent and of Grenada, namely outer islands that use the stamps of the home country for postal purposes, but produce large numbers of pictorial issues for sale to collectors. A listing of all new issues for 1987 showed over 200 stamps and miniature sheets from Guyana, Grenada and the African country of Guinea.

These are the major offenders. Stanley Gibbons lists countries whose issues, it believes, are essentially intended for foreign collectors in a special appendix. As they wrote of a large series of stamps produced for Afghanistan in the early 1960s, "It became evident that token supplies were only placed on sale in Kabul for a few hours and some of these sets contained stamps of very low denominations for which there was no possible postal use."[3] Perhaps the most egregious offender is the island of Redonda, a dependency of the West Indies state of Antigua, which has no population and no post office of its own, but which has had an active stamp-producing program since 1979. Countries such as Mongolia and Vietnam have a two-part program of stamp issues, one for domestic use and the other exclusively for foreign consumption. On the other hand, not all Third World countries are prolific in their stamp production — Burma and Nigeria have been as restrained as Norway and Denmark.

The rewards of philatelic sales are considerable, and a major budget item for a number of countries, including the postal services of the Vatican and the United Nations. It is estimated that the United Nations makes $10 million a year from postal sales, even though its stamps can only be used at one post office in the United Nations building in New York. This is topped up by sales of (different) UN stamps in Geneva and Vienna, as well as specific stamps for UNESCO and some international agencies with headquarters in Geneva. The hard currency rewards explain why local designs and topics are far less likely to appear on stamps from Bhutan, Gabon and the Turks and Caicos Islands than are European art, American history and the ubiquitous British Royals. In 1983 the Pacific island state of Tuvalu sold over $600,000 worth of stamps, more than it received in foreign exchange from its major export, copra. Equally, the Australian territory of Christmas Island, with a population of 3000, takes in over half a million dollars from stamp sales, largely to collectors.

In many cases, stamps designed exclusively for the collectors' market are identifiable from their content. Why else would Hungary issue stamps, in 1981, showing paintings of the American illustrator Norman Rockwell? Perhaps the best known (and most ubiquitous) are stamps designed by the Walt Disney studios, who have designed issues for such surprising clients as Mongolia and Romania. Since the end of the 1950s, a few firms in the First World have specialised in producing and marketing stamps for poor, small Third World countries, which increasingly look more like glossy stickers than any conventional notion of stamps.

Despite denials from the countries concerned, it is clear that the agencies often dictate the subject matter and designs of their stamps. Such agencies have their predecessor in a 19th-century businessman, Seebeck, who arranged to produce stamps for several Latin American countries in return for the right to retain all those left over, as well as the printing plates, so that he could print more copies when the original lot did not satisfy collectors' demands.

Modern agencies are more ingenious in swelling philatelic revenues. Increasingly, stamp production agencies seek new markets and new outlets for their products. In recent years there have been supermarket campaigns to sell certain stamps, such as those issued for the 1987 America's Cup, or a series of stamps, 81 in all, showing American baseball players from Grenada. How far removed from any postal purpose

SOLOMON ISLANDS 1987

these stamps have become is demonstrated by the report that, "The idea for the baseball issue was orchestrated by the Inter-Governmental Philatelic Corp of New York, philatelic agents for the Grenada Post Office; International Philatelic Corp; Grenada Post Office; and officials of Major League Baseball and the Major League Baseball Players Association".[4]

The largest agency is the Crown Agents, originally founded as a purchasing agent for the British colonies which now oversees the production of stamps for some 50 states, not all of them British or ex-British colonies. Most imaginative is probably the Inter-Governmental Philatelic Corp, which in addition to the above example has produced stamps issued by several states simultaneously showing contemporary tennis stars, and an issue — from Gambia, but this seems irrelevant — showing such "famous entertainers of the past" as Yul Brynner, Fred Astaire and Ginger Rogers and Jackie Gleeson, alongside other stars of the 1950s television series *The Honeymooners*.

In at least one case a philatelic agency has been implicated in directly meddling in the political affairs of its client country. In 1978 the High Court of the Cook Islands, an autonomous group of Pacific islands associated with New Zealand, unseated the 13-year-old government of Sir Albert "Papa" Henry after allegations that the New York based Cook

Islands Philatelic and Numismatic Bureau had provided money as an advance against philatelic revenue for charter flights of voters from New Zealand to help re-elect Henry. The head of the Bureau, Finbar Kenny, was charged under the United States Foreign Corrupt Practises Act, and an agreement between the US and the Cook Islands required him to reimburse the money that had been spent.[5] Kenny presumably no longer runs the stamp business of the Islands, but they continue to be among the most prolific issuers of stamps in the region.

The Hobby

"Rupert, what are you thinking of?"
"I was just thinking of all the years I wasted collecting
stamps." Groucho Marx, *Duck Soup*

Within a few years of the first stamp appearing, people began collecting them. In 1842 one lady advertised in *The Times* asking for Penny Blacks to wallpaper her room. This was a craze that persisted. A letter from the writer Vita Sackville-West to *The Times* in 1956 recalled that in the months before her birth, in 1892, "My mother amused herself... by papering a small room at Knowle with stamps arranged in strips and patterns... I remember there were many Russian stamps of the Tsarist regime and there were some early Victorian stamps also."[6]

By 1862 one report claimed that many older stamps (at most 22 years old) already cost 100 times their original value.[7] The term "philatelist", based on two Greek words meaning "love" and "free from tax", was coined by a Frenchman, George Herpin, in 1865. Within a few decades the first philatelic clubs, magazines and catalogues had all come into existence.[8] The 19th century saw collecting of all kinds become extremely popular, both in the creation of public museums and art galleries, and as a hobby of the middle classes. As Donald Horne observed of the new craze, "The stamp album is itself a kind of do-it-yourself museum, involving classification, catalogues… auctions, dreams of unexpected finds and tests of authenticity."[9]

Stamp collecting became very popular by the end of the 19th century, and became known as "the hobby of Kings and the king of hobbies" because of the patronage of collectors such as King George V, King Farouk of Egypt and, most famous of all, President Franklin Roosevelt, whose interest in stamps was well known. Estimates of the numbers of collectors vary enormously, but one article in the staid journal *The Accountant* claimed it would be between 50 and 100 million world wide.[10] Stamp collecting is generally regarded as second only to photography as the world's most popular hobby.

Most collectors would not qualify for the title "philatelist", which should strictly be applied to those who study as well as assemble stamps. Philatelists take themselves extremely seriously, with various official national bodies and

RWANDA 1970

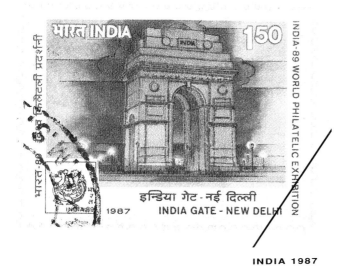

INDIA 1987

an international Roll of Distinguished Philatelists, administered by the British Philatelic Federation. Stamp collecting had been a British invention, and as one observer noted, "Victorian Philately, lest we are tempted to forget, [was] — as it is today — a pursuit of middle and upper-class gentlemen, headed at one end by the Prince of Wales who became George V and at the other by various clerks and professionals of various degrees."[11] To enter the centres of organised philately, such as the BPF or the Collectors' Club in New York, is to enter an archaic world of club-gentlemen, where small groups sit around old tables discussing such topics as "plating the Saorstat Overprints". (This is the title of a three-page article in the edition of *Stamps* referred to in note 11.) Indeed French resentment of the British domination of philately led to the creation of the Federation Internationale de Philatélie, which authorises official international stamp exhibitions in member countries. One recent show, INDIA 89, was opened by the President of the Republic and visited by 50,000 people. Every ten years, by tradition, there is a major exhibition in London, coinciding with the decennial anniversaries of the first stamp.

A very large number of stamp clubs and associations exist, even if most of their members would never aim for inclusion on the Distinguished Roll. The scale of the hobby can be seen by examining any of the major philatelic magazines that regularly list scores of local stamp clubs, ranging from neighbourhood groups to clubs devoted to specialised topics and study groups. One of the largest is the American Topical Association, which claims over 10,000 members in 90 countries, and caters for collectors interested in special themes; it contains scores of sub-groups with their own publications, with names like *Scalpel and Tongs* (medicine on stamps) and *Curtain Call* (theatre on stamps). The range of topics that philatelists explore — many of them, such as perforations, watermarks and printing techniques not touched upon in this book — can be gleaned from the fact that one bibliography of philatelic articles for Canada alone has 5772 entries for the period 1864–1983.

Not surprisingly, philately appears best organised in West Germany, where there is a whole hierarchy of stamp exhibitions controlled by the Federation of German Philatelists. It also enjoys considerable status in Eastern Europe. When Gorbachev's reforms led to the election in 1989 of 750 members representing "public associations" to the Congress of People's Deputies, the Association of Stamp Collectors was one group represented.[12]

The rhetoric used about stamp collecting is that it cuts across class, race and other barriers, but this is hardly true, least of all in terms of gender. The first collectors seem to have been women, but collecting soon became largely a male preserve, and some philatelic societies long excluded women from membership. In recent years there has been some discussion in the philatelic world about the reason stamp collecting is such a male preoccupation, little of it particularly enlightened.[13] The standard explanation, at least of middle-class British collectors, is summed up in the early pages of Robert Graves' novel *Antigua, Penny, Puce*, almost certainly the most entertaining book ever written around the hobby:

> *All British schoolboys of a certain age collect postage-stamps or at least all schoolboys whose parents have a little money; below a certain social level the collecting instinct must, we suppose, be satisfied largely with cigarette pictures and gift coupons. Schoolgirls, on the other hand ... do not go in for stamp collecting. In fact they usually despise the pursuit, which is not direct and personal to satisfy them emotionally: if they collect anything it is signed photographs of famous actors and actresses.*[14]

This was written in 1936. The snobbishness, the class and sex prejudices, tell us a lot about why stamp collecting, at least in Britain, is not genuinely universal. But of course, collecting is not confined to British middle-class men. Stamp collectors can be found in all societies where there are people literate enough to be in touch with a mail system. My impression is that most stamp collectors have above average education, if not incomes, are fairly conservative, at least

UNITED STATES OF AMERICA 1986

socially, and largely hostile to suggestions that there is a political dimension to stamp collecting.

Almost all children will collect something at some point in their lives, even if only spasmodically. There is a certain amount of psychological literature on children's collecting habits, which tends to agree that it peaks in the immediate pre-adolescence years and that it has declined over the past several decades — for which all sorts of reasons are given, including television, video games, greater disposable incomes and the breakdown of the traditional family. Less has been written about the collecting habits of adults, although it is clearly linked to the "possessive individualism" that became the dominant value system of bourgeois society in the 18th and 19th centuries. Just why people collect, why they collect stamps (as against, say, matchboxes or antique clocks) and why stamp-collecting becomes so obsessional for so many, is less clear.

The clichés are that stamp collecting attracts people because it introduces them to geography, history and "the customs and achievements of other countries". As one book, published by a stamp firm, put it, "Families find stamps a wonderful way to spend time together... through stamps... we grow in our understanding of foreign lands and people."[15] Such clichés seem to me to often verge on nonsense. My favourite example comes from Bill Hornadge's book, *Stamps: A Collector's Guide*, which extols collecting as "a vital factor in curbing delinquency and channelling youthful exuberance into creative channels". On the opposite page he shows two stamps illustrating this argument, one of which was issued by the Nazi puppet government of Slovakia.[16] Hornadge also claims that some Eastern European countries have, in the past, imposed considerable restrictions on stamp collecting, and banned altogether the collection of stamps that are considered subversive because they showed, for example, a portrait of Hitler. Equally, the United States maintains a ban on the import and sale of the stamps of a number of Communist countries.

I suspect one of the great attractions of collecting stamps is that, however many they are, they are also finite; because they are produced by governments, they can be catalogued, and one can aspire to a certain degree of completeness in a given collection. (It has been suggested to me that stamp collecting is a symbolic way of mastering the external world, and that this is a particularly male obsession.) It is probably true that stamp collecting does lead to a greater knowledge of history and geography. Who but a historian or a stamp collector could identify Dedeagach, Morvi or Fezzan? (Respectively, a seaport in western Greece under the control of various powers and with stamps produced by a French post office between 1874 and 1914; a former feudatory state, now part of the Gujarat province of India; the south-eastern portion of Libya, which issued stamps during its occupation by the French during and after World War II.) As Justice Frankfurter wrote to that great stamp collector, Franklin Roosevelt, "These two sets of stamps are a meagre offer to you for extending the bounds of my geography. I now know, and I am not likely ever to forget, that Lithuania is Lithuania, and Besserabia is Besserabia, and never the twain shall meet. Lithuania is Lithuania; but the only philatelic recognition of Besserabia I have been able to find is a Rumanian issue of 1928 celebrating Besserabia's declaration of independence from Russia in 1918, and while Besserabia is no longer independent, the one leu and two leu stamps at least teach me that there is a Besserabian Parliament House." [17]

I would agree with the comments made over 50 years ago by the editor of the Gibbons' Catalogue that, "There is glamour [in] being in touch with the end of the earth, the romance of . . . stamps which reflect very rapidly a revolution in South America, the death of a king, an earthquake, or a royal wedding.''[18] But it seems to me remarkably naive to conclude that greater knowledge leads to greater harmony. The Nazis were quite keen on stamp collecting and regularly issued stamps for Stamp Day.

The Stamp Trade

It's now getting near the point where they're collecting money and we're collecting labels. Hunter Davies *The Joy of Stamps*

Almost as soon as the habit of collecting stamps emerged, so too did the business of supplying stamps to collectors. There are records of stamp dealers existing in London, Paris, Brussels, Liverpool and New York by the 1860s. The most famous was Edward Stanley Gibbons, who began dealing in his father's chemist shop in Plymouth in 1856, then moved to London and founded what is still probably the largest stamp business in the world. Gibbons moved his business to the Strand in London, which became the centre of London's stamp business, rather like Nassau Street in New York and the area round the Bourse in Paris. Nassau Street has lost most of its shops, but the area around the Strand still has a large number of dealers.

Gibbons became best known for his catalogue, which first appeared in 1863 and, with the American Scott, since 1868, and several European catalogues, remains the major world reference to stamps, with sales of up to 100,000 annually. Gibbons, like other stamp firms, also produces a

whole range of philatelic literature and accessories, and is a
major auction house.

The stamp business is essentially a large collection
of very small businesses which, as far as I can discover, has
never been seriously studied. One survey, by the American
Stamp Dealers' Association in 1976, estimated that the total
business in the United States had a turnover of over one billion
US dollars per year. What is striking in this study is that most
dealers are very small — almost half the firms surveyed had
annual sales of under $50,000 — and that mail order sales were
much the largest category of activity. Stamp dealing is an
excellent cottage industry, which is adopted by many people
on retirement (my own fantasies about retirement sometimes
involve a Dickensian-style stamp shop where I can sell off the
accumulation of a lifetime). As the study concluded:

> *The typical stamp dealer is a 49 year old white man...*
> *trained as an engineer but his love of stamp collecting*
> *competed with his profession and in his late thirties he*
> *became a full-time professional stamp dealer... He runs*
> *his business as a sole proprieter, often with his wife's*
> *help since his children have grown up and left home.*
> *With one full-time employee and occasionally a part-*
> *time helper, he solicits stamps through the mail in*
> *addition to his small retail store.*[19]

In some countries, a significant number of stamp
dealers are Jewish, and some people have argued to me that
stamp collecting is a very Jewish pursuit. Its internationalism,
and the portability of collections, appeals to people who
historically have moved frequently from country to country.
This theory may explain why the only recorded stamp-dealer
in Ethiopia during the days of Emperor Haile Selassie was an
Armenian. As the American collector, Viola Ilma, founder of

**AUSTRIA 1960;
THAILAND 1973**

the American Youth Congress (whose first introduction to stamps came from President Roosevelt) recalled:

His shop [was] down a muddy alley. The sign outside said "Photography" because he thought that looked classier than "Stamps". He sat between stacks of unlabeled boxes, studying stamps laid out on the arms of his chair. Every so often he had a coughing fit and thousands of dollars in stamps blew around the room. He didn't talk much but, baby, he did know his oats.[20]

Stamp collectors can be found in almost every country. By the 1930s, philatelic magazines existed in Japanese, Chinese and Persian, as well as most European languages. In some European and South American cities there are regular open-air markets where both dealers and collectors gather to sell and swap. When I lived in Paris I would often spend a couple of hours at the edge of the Champs-Elysées where the market gathered, searching out elusive stamps, and occasionally finding dealers who would accept used Australian stamps in return for their own stock.

Postal authorities themselves have become major players in the stamp trade, with those of Canada, Sweden and Australia among the world's most innovative. As far back as 1921, the United States Post Office had established a special agency to promote sales to collectors, and it was the boast of Franklin Roosevelt's Postmaster General, James Farley, that the popularity of the hobby was expanded enormously during his administration. By 1938 he claimed there were nine million American collectors and the Post Office was making almost $2 million from their purchases.[21]

The unveiling in 1989 of a set of four stamps depicting dinosaurs at Universal City Studios, itself about to issue on video a film featuring dinosaurs, shows the attempts that are increasingly being made to sell stamps outside conventional philatelic markets.

AUSTRALIA 1985

Post offices themselves no longer sell only stamps. Each new issue comes with first day covers, special packs and sometimes commemorative books or maps, all of which make tidy profits for them. The main post office in Paris markets stamps from various French dependencies as well as Monaco and Andorra. In philatelic agencies in Australia and New Zealand one can buy stamps from half a dozen Pacific islands. Post offices have become major sponsors of stamp collecting, with large numbers of stamps issued to encourage the hobby. Since a resolution of the International Federation of Philately in 1936, a number of countries, primarily European, have issued stamps for "Stamp Day", and there exist numerous special issues for stamp exhibitions and competitions (see at left). The New Zealand national stamp exhibition of 1986 saw not only special stamps and covers, but also souvenir cards, pens and badges.

In a number of capital cities there are national postal museums, run by the post office, the best known of which are probably in Paris, Stockholm and the Hague. Marketing of stamps is increasingly a major activity of post offices, who are keenly aware of the revenue that collectors can generate. The US Postal Service has used full page advertisements for stamp collecting in glossy magazines and in 1989, the British Post Office followed suit. One of Australia Post's most successful issues involved the reprinting of five classic Australian children's books by a commercial publisher in conjunction with a special stamp issue (see previous page). Nearly a million copies of the books were sold. Australia Post was less successful with a series of stamps prepared to celebrate an Australian victory in the yacht race, the America's Cup, in 1987. The stamps, which were overprints of the set issued after Australia won the race in 1983, had to be pulped when the Cup was, in fact, won back by the United States. By the time of the Bicentennial celebrations of 1988, Australia Post was making over $42 million from its philatelic operations, less than half of this from the direct sale of stamps, and being criticised by some collectors for over-production.

There is still room for an expansion of marketing, particularly if post offices explore further the possibility of using stamps as an advertising device. The link between stamps and advertising goes back to the 19th century, when some halfpenny British stamps showing Queen Victoria had the words "Pears' Soap" overprinted across the back. New Zealand allowed such advertisements for some time, and earlier this century both Italy and Belgium experimented with selling advertising space on pieces of paper attached to stamps. One can still find stamps attached to small notices for Campari and Singer sewing machines. While this is no longer done, many countries issue stamp booklets that contain considerable amounts of advertising and postal promotion. There is one Hungarian stamp booklet, issued in 1984, that contains recipes.

The line between direct advertising and influencing stamp content becomes a fine one in some of the Disney stamps, or in the series produced for a large range of British colonies and dominions, marking the tercentenary of the insurance house, Lloyd's of London. Today, in the United

Silver items from Lloyd's Nelson Collection

FALKLAND ISLANDS

FALKLAND ISLANDS 1988

States, one can buy packs of stamps in supermarkets which carry with them an array of store coupons and special offers. The US Post Office seems unconcerned about who markets its stamps, and has traditionally had a more flexible policy (allowing, for example, private vending machines to sell stamps) than most countries.

Stamps as Investments

Most people who do not collect stamps have a very inflated idea of their worth. As one finance writer put it,

> *Think back to that kid down the block who was too busy poring over his stamp collection to play baseball. Did you ever wonder what happened to him?*
>
> *He might have retired at 55 to the Sun Belt, after selling his collection for $400,000. An American collector recently sold his stamp 'collection' for about $10 million.*[22]

If that kid sold his collection for one-tenth this amount, it would almost certainly have been a collection he kept going in adult life, and one that involved considerable judicious purchases over the years. The reality is that the great bulk of stamps around, and in childhood collections, are worth very little; this is why they were easily obtained in the first place. One of the most common myths about stamp collections is, that if they contain old stamps they are valuable. The sad reality is that most old collections are basically made up of stamps that were issued in their millions, and are unlikely to be saleable, except in cheap job lots, which bear very little resemblance to the catalogue value of the stamps. Where old collections do appear to contain valuable stamps, they are very often forgeries. Some of the classical issues, for example, from Heligoland, an island in the North Sea under British control between 1807 and 1890, when it passed to Germany, were reprinted in large numbers by commercial dealers who got possession of the plates, and are therefore largely worthless.

There is a crucial difference between rarity and value. Many stamps with low catalogue prices are hard to get hold of. Others, which are much more expensive, can be quite easily obtained, although they may involve watching the catalogues of stamp dealers and auctioneers. The difference is clearly one of demand and supply. The rarest stamp is worth nothing if no one collects it. Nonetheless, very valuable stamps do, of course, exist, and can be worth a great deal. The record price — over a million dollars — was paid in 1987 by a Japanese Bank for an 1852 US local stamp, known as "Lady McGill". The previous record was held by the British Guyana 1856 one cent, which has itself been portrayed on a stamp.[23] The Guyana stamp remains a stamp legend, one copy having been held by several famous collectors, especially the French

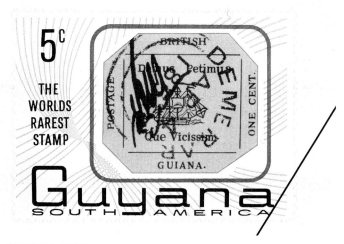

GUYANA 1967

eccentric Ferrary, from whose collection it passed at the end of World War I, for over £7,000, to the American Arthur Hind.[24] Stamp prices fluctuate considerably with fashion but even so, a study of investments over the period 1975–85 showed that rare stamps outperformed all other investments except for coins and Chinese ceramics. There was a boom during the 1970s, followed by the inevitable slump. Nonetheless, at the end of the 1980s stamp values seemed to be moving up again, with stamp magazines full of news of record auction prices and tips to investors.

The problem is, of course, to determine what will be in demand. Apart from a few hundred famous issues, rare either because very few were ever issued, as with the Guyana example or the first Hawaiian stamps, known as "missionaries" because they were used almost exclusively by foreign clerics, or because there are errors, such as inverted centres or missing colours, there are large numbers of stamps whose values appear to fluctuate dramatically according to changing fashions. As collectors tend to specialise in the stamps of their own country, there is a premium on stamps from rich countries, or from countries with particular ties to them. British collectors force up the value of Commonwealth stamps, Catholic and Jewish Americans are often attracted to the stamps of Ireland, the Vatican and Israel.

1. Angelo Loukakis, "The Royal Arcade", *Good Weekend*, 18 March 1988.
2. P. Thorp, *A Guide to Stamp Collecting*, Minkus, New York, 1972, p. 19.
3. *Stanley Gibbons' Stamps of the World*, London, 1985, p. 7.
4. *Linn's Stamp News*, 12 December 1988.
5. S. Inder, "Fall of the House of Henry", *Pacific Islands Monthly*, September 1978, pp. 11–12; and "The wash-up of the Cooks' conspiracy trial", *Pacific Islands Monthly*, October 1979, pp. 20–2.
6. K. Gregory, *The Last Cuckoo: The Very Best Letters to* The Times, Unwin Hyman, London, 1987, p. 64.
7. Neil Grant and Peter Womersley, *Collecting Stamps*, Granada, London, 1980, p. 41.
8. For details see L.N. and M. Williams, *The Postage Stamp*, Penguin, Harmondsworth, 1956, pp. 52–58.

9. D. Horne, *The Great Museum*, Pluto, London, 1984, p. 15.

10. "You Can't Lick Stamps", *The Accountant*, 31 July 1980, p. 180.

11. Edgar Lewis, "Views on the News", *Stamps*, vol. 8, no. 10, 1988. p. 12.

12. S. Handelman, "Slav Passions Rise to Western Election Hype", the *Australian*, 22 March 1989.

13. See for example Hunter Davies, *The Joy of Stamps*, Robson, London, 1983, pp. 106-9.

14. R. Graves, *Antigua, Penny, Puce*, Penguin, Harmondsworth, 1968, p. 8.

15. P. Thorp, *op cit*, pp. 7-8.

16. B. Hornadge, *Stamps: A Collector's Guide*, Sun Books, Melbourne, 1968, pp. 24-5.

17. Letter of 20 November 1934 in *Roosevelt and Frankfurter: Their Correspondence*, annotated by Max Freedman, Little Brown, Boston, 1967, p. 244.

18. S. Phillips, *Stamp Collecting*, Sampson Low, London, 1932, p. 278.

19. ASDA Membership Questionnaire, September 1976.

20. K. Leishman, "Topical Fever", *Connoisseur*, August 1984, p. 92.

21. James Farley, *Behind the Ballts*, Harcourt, Brace, New York, 1938, p. 258.

22. Bruce Stone, "Stamps: A bull market for 50 years", *Commodities*, August 1980, p. 41.

23. Hunter Davies, "Moaning About Money", *Stamps*, vol. 8, no. 10, 1988, p. 20.

24. See Grant and Womersley, *op cit*, pp. 107-8.

CONCLUSION:

THE FUTURE OF STAMPS

It is ironic that as stamps proliferate, fewer and fewer are being used for postal purposes. Various forms of electronic mail and courier services are eroding the use of the postage stamp, while stamps themselves become bigger, gaudier and appear more frequently. Yet, even as postage meters, FAX machines and private couriers replace more traditional ways of sending mail, and as a number of countries move towards "privatisation" of more aspects of communications, it is highly unlikely that the government monopoly over stamp production will be relinquished. This would currently be impossible under UPU regulations, but it is also true that no government would willingly give up the potential propaganda and revenue benefits of controlling stamp production.

Nonetheless, it is likely that by the end of the century, the majority of countries will have joined those, such as Bhutan, Djibouti, the various small states of the Caribbean and the Pacific, whose stamps go straight from the printing presses of London and New York to collectors, and are not even available to the countries that allegedly issue them. As this happens the appearance of stamps will become more and more interchangeable, and the dominance of Atlantic-centric designs, aimed at the schoolkids and the collectors of the First World, more significant. To date, however, there have been more than enough stamps that represent both the conscious and the unconscious agendas of governments to make them worth exploring for hints of how states see the world, and how they wish to be seen.

INDEX

References to stamps are italicised.